"This book is a meaningful and important contribution to the work of coaches. Sherene has provided a definitive roadmap that will guide me going forward."

Dave Riddle
Randolph Stanton Leadership Consulting

"This important book adds Sherene Zolno's unique voice to those of our most respected mentors – those who share the knowledge-base of master coaches. What she's taught me is integral to who I have become as a coach, leader and guide."

Everett Marshall
Forest, TLC

"A magical must read for any coach from any field who is dedicated to taking their coaching practice to the next level."

Jim Haley
Signature Impact Coaching

"Filled with amazing stories, insights, and practical applications – Sherene generously shares thirty years of knowledge and experience with us. Read this book closely!"

Larry Ransom
The Synergy Network

"The theories, models and ideas Sherene's put together are nothing short of brilliant! They're taking me to a new level of understanding."

Sonja Price
Dynamo Careers

ALIGN

A COACH'S GUIDE

Sherene Zolno

ARCHWAY
PUBLISHING

This book is a work of non-fiction. Unless otherwise noted, the author and the publisher make no explicit guarantees as to the accuracy of the information contained in this book and in some cases, names of people and places have been altered to protect their privacy.

Archway Publishing books may be ordered through booksellers or by contacting:

Archway Publishing
1663 Liberty Drive
Bloomington, IN 47403
www.archwaypublishing.com
844-669-3957

ISBN: 978-1-6657-0051-1 (sc)
ISBN: 978-1-6657-0052-8 (e)

Library of Congress Control Number: 2020925141

Print information available on the last page.

Archway Publishing rev. date: 01/23/2021

To my colleagues, teachers, students and clients who have stretched and moved me.

To my sister Rose who is always ready to listen.

And to Rick, my Lief. You are my forever inspiration.

"We are participants in a vast communion of being, and if we open ourselves to its guidance, we can learn anew how to live in this great and gracious community of truth."

– Parker Palmer

Dedicated to you

I didn't think I would write a book. I adamantly said I wouldn't. I changed my mind.

I wrote this book because I believe that you, who have responded to the calling of being a coach, deserve to have access to whatever knowledge I have acquired in my more than 40 years in this field, as a coach, consultant, researcher, author, educator, mentor, trainer and organization development professional. You are the reason why I have dedicated this past year to writing this book.

If you are like my other coaching colleagues, I know that you are highly principled. You are a deep vessel for compassion. I have seen, heard about and felt the results of your dedication, as I have experienced my own. Like me, you are hardworking and committed to making the world a better place to live in. You are contributing your knowledge and wisdom to building a better, more fruitful and productive life at work, and in homes and communities around the world. It seems that together we are on a sacred mission to improve the world around us.

I am grateful that being an educator as well as a coach has allowed me to inspire others. I am grateful to have met students, other coaches and colleagues, and yes, my family and my clients as well, who inspire me. As one coach, my friend, Dave, said to me recently, "Coaching for me is more than being a facilitator or working with an executive team. Coaching is an invitation into the very personal world of another human being."[1]

He reminded me that our work as coaches includes "sitting in the fire"[2] with our clients, holding the space for hope and for a better life for them (and for ourselves as well). As a result of our conversations, we want our clients to "rise like a phoenix" from the fire that is their life, to journey from darkness to light, as they align their world with the positive possibilities we will discover in our work together. And I find that as my clients can be vulnerable, so can I. And, like the great coaches I have met, I also strive to be present for whatever comes, be it tears of pain or tears of joy, theirs, and mine.

I have found it exciting, though, to see that our field has advanced to the forefront of human development. In our coaching we are free to blend findings from neuroscience, positive psychology, action research, organizational theory, and even ancient wisdom traditions. We add this to our own insights and intuition to create new approaches to human growth.

This book, *ALIGN, a Coach's Guide,* is intended to add to your coaching toolbox a meaningful set of ideas and models that work. I also, however, hope to ignite a renewed commitment to doing deep coaching with clients and client systems – the kind of coaching that grows a sense of self-worth, hope and capability in our clients and the people they touch. This is what will make a difference in the quality of their lives. And ours.

That, to me, means supporting others to align their lives with their vision – doing *whole* work, applying a new form of coaching intelligence. I call this approach WS *IQ*, Whole System Intelligence. I have found that WS *IQ*, introduced here and in the training programs I have held for over twenty-five years to certify coaches around the world, is the path I've traveled leading to system alignment and transformation.

You are most welcome to travel it with me.

CONTENTS

ALIGN

A Coach's Guide

Introduction and Overview

Introduction to *ALIGN, a Coach's Guide*

Bringing the dream of the future into the present. Coaching Whole Systems.

In off-sites and team meetings all over the world where vision and mission conversations are being held nearly every day (somewhere!), we may well wonder why leaders, with their numerous consultants and coaches, haven't yet perfected the process for how to align what they are doing in their enterprises with what they need to be doing to get what they want. Instead, misalignments occur at every level and in all sorts of processes, and, most disheartening of all, between what people envision they could be when at their best, in fact yearn for and dream of, and their day-to-day work-life.

So what's the hold-up?

Psychologists point out five powerful wants in people:

> People want to do the right thing.
> People want to find better ways of doing things.
> People want to achieve things of which they can be proud.
> People want to belong to a group that achieves the extraordinary.
> And they want to earn respect and recognition for who they are
> and for what they achieve.

These wants are my wants. They are what led me to join the international community of coaches and consultants. As a coach I have sought to collaborate with clients to create environments that allow human needs to be met, that allow them to align their lives with their dreams. I have learned that we can only do that well by doing *whole* work, work that is broad and deep and considers what's going on in the whole system. Whole System Intelligence, or WS *IQ*, Whole Field Alignment, or *WFA*, and the ALIGN Coaching process, or *LEAD*, were developed to guide coaches in that work.

ALIGN Coaching: Aligning with Vision

From the perspective of many years of research, teaching and coaching, I would suggest that the misalignments that constrain people's workplace joy and engagement aren't people problems. Instead, they are systems issues.

Like Trevor and Varcoe[3], I have long believed that misalignments are the result of not understanding the whole system and of having no one with the accountability or responsibility for *seeing* the system, focusing on understanding the complexity of it, and ensuring alignment within it and with it and other systems.

In fact, many efforts to transform organizations through mergers and acquisitions, restructuring, improving processes or strategy work falter because we fail to grasp what it really takes to shift and sustain change throughout a system. We will counter this weakness in our coaching by understanding Whole System Intelligence, and by applying the tools for change found in Whole Field Alignment and LEAD. By bringing forward this form of intelligence, called WS *IQ* – Whole System Intelligence, I believe you will multiply your impact as a coach and extend the influence of your clients who are hungry to make a positive difference in their world.

I am delighted, therefore, to introduce coaches, and those who utilize coaching skills, to *ALIGN, a Coach's Guide* because it is designed to expand our understanding of how to integrate vision into our lives – in other words, how to align our lives with the hopes and dreams we have for ourselves. In it I present models and processes that will enable coaches to assist leaders and stakeholders of systems, small to large, to assess and understand the interrelated components of the systems in which they live and work. Most importantly, this book contains specific, practical and tested actions you can take to start immediately engaging clients in aligning their everyday reality with their imagined and hoped for future.

With the ideas and the specific steps towards transforming a system that are described in *ALIGN, a Coach's Guide*, you and your clients can walk the path to alignment knowing you have the theoretical and practical support needed for every stage of the journey.

In *ALIGN, a Coach's Guide* you will learn:

- The foundation: the Six Components of ALIGN Coaching.

  1. **FRAME THE CONVERSATION**

  2. **STRENGTHEN THE CORE:** self-worth, hope and capability

  3. **TELL YOUR VISION STORY**

  4. **GENERATE POSSIBILITY**

  5. **ALIGN OPERATIONS and ESTABLISH A LEAD TEAM**

  6. **TEACH PROCESS ALIGNMENT**

- **The new human intelligence model (It's the coach's secret!): WS *IQ* – Whole System Intelligence.**

- **Systems thinking that makes sense: WFA – Whole Field Alignment.**

- **The four phases of ALIGN Coaching – LEAD.**

  1. **LEARN**

  2. **ENVISION**

  3. **ALIGN**

  4. **DELIVER**

Overview of ALIGN Coaching

Have you heard about the coach who loves to help his clients create a vision – it makes him feel 'high' – but then he thinks his client engagement, and the change work, is done?

Or about the consultants who in focus group interviews listened to employees say over and over (and over) that they had no clear idea of what their job should entail, but then proposed a one-day teambuilding session as the solution? Or, after employees continued to complain, proposed an off-the-shelf Lean or Continuous Improvement training so everyone could join in to "fix" the company's "problems"?

Or the tale of one coach who thinks her job is only to observe people at work for a few days and then report in on what she's seen or heard to the boss, her client?

Like me, you may have heard plenty of accounts like these about well-paid coaches and consultants that are shortchanging their clients. They are not "hearing" focus group input, or, from the start, may have been seeking only to sell their own training programs. They provide incomplete services that lack systems understanding. They often fail to make a difference, and their work fades away.

We need to get smarter!

Peter Block once wrote, "The whole system is your client. All parts of it need to be supported, to learn and to be fully informed."[4] However, structuring a change process to align a whole system is a new knowledge arena for most of us coaches and our clients. I believe we urgently need to get smarter about it!

ALIGN Coaching supports you as you gain expertise and skills in this new knowledge arena, gives you a step-by-step guide to making change applying this whole system approach, and shows you how to customize your whole system change designs to be responsive to your clients' cultures and needs.

The Six components of ALIGN

Part One of *ALIGN, a Coach's Guide* introduces the six components that form the foundation for ALIGN Coaching. These six components include the core values and beliefs that guide ALIGN Coaching as well as actions that need to be taken in aligning a whole system. They indicate the knowledge, attitudes, capabilities and skills you will need to be the kind of coach that can facilitate ALIGN Coaching. Put together, these six build perceptions and attitudes that make possible engaging your clients in processes for aligning with vision.

The six components of ALIGN are:

1. **FRAME THE CONVERSATION**

2. **STRENGTHEN THE CORE: self-worth, hope and capability**

3. **TELL YOUR VISION STORY**

4. **GENERATE POSSIBILITY**

5. **ALIGN OPERATIONS and ESTABLISH A LEAD TEAM**

6. **TEACH PROCESS ALIGNMENT**

These six components of ALIGN Coaching are covered in Part One.

In addition, ALIGN is further covered in Part Two, Whole System Intelligence, in the discussion of Whole Field Alignment; and in Part Three, Coaching Your Client Through LEAD, in the discussion of ALIGN.

The word LEAD is an acronym for the four phases of whole system change: LEARN, ENVISION, ALIGN and DELIVER.

WS IQ – Whole System Intelligence

WS *IQ* is a mental ability found in individuals that enables coaching and leading a whole system. A coach and a leader with high WS *IQ* who are engaged in a multiple entry, system-wide change process can expect to have an exceptionally impactful and sustainable outcome.

ALIGN COACHING

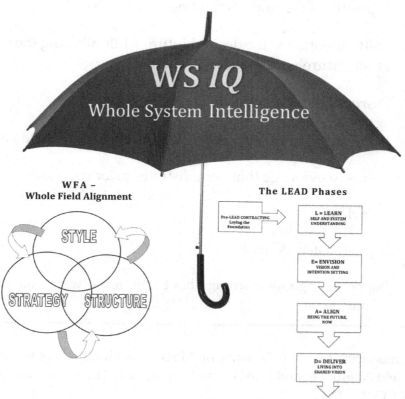

It might be helpful to think of WS *IQ* as the umbrella under which are two approaches (methodologies) for achieving sustainable, whole system change – change that can be imagined, planned, and delivered. **The methodologies within WS *IQ* that coaches need to better understand and deploy more effectively are 1) Whole Field Alignment (WFA) and 2) LEAD.**

ALIGN, a Coach's Guide presents these as the coach's essential and indispensable tools for helping clients get a handle on what is going on in their systems. With them, coaches and their clients can effect *well-formed* change.

A change is said to be well-formed if it:

- Considers and involves the whole system.

- Is positive, bold and compelling.

- Shifts attention to the desired future while aligning the vision of the future with present-day actions.

- Disrupts the status quo.

- Is grounded in the system's strengths and deeply-held values.

- Points to evidence that demonstrates prior successes.

- Is inclusive.

- Is passionately desired;

- Supports ongoing learning about how to be what you always wanted to be.

The interconnectedness of the parts of ALIGN Coaching – Whole System *IQ*, Whole Field Alignment and LEAD – can be understood by using the illustration "ALIGN COACHING".

This graphic shows that for whole system alignment to occur there is an over-arching necessity for WS *IQ*. Without a comprehensive understanding of and connection with all significant aspects of the system, planned changes won't have their intended impact. Some action, inaction or reaction to the change is likely to occur in a part of the system that hadn't been considered during the planning stages for change. The result we've often seen before: attempted changes came and went, and the dream of the future was not fulfilled.

I have met with groups of supervisors and employees in several organizations that confessed that they "just wait awhile, and the latest change fad will just fade away." Studs Terkel, in his book *WORKING*[5], after a series of interviews with working people from all over the country, quoted one person as saying, "If my ideas are discounted, I just tell the organization what it wants to hear. I'm no longer engaged in the outcome." Comments like this are a sure indicator of a growing potential for change apathy and a backlash in one part of the system to a proposed change in another.

In the ALIGN Coaching approach the Whole System *IQ* that is needed is achieved by having a model for understanding the whole system (Whole Field Alignment), and by linking that to a process for engaging the whole system in creating a new future (LEAD). With these interlinked approaches to whole system change, learning stays within the system and deepens the sense of community. This is what makes possible extensive engagement and the involvement of our clients with multiple stakeholders, while showing faith in people's capacity to find ways to address barriers to achieving their vision. ALIGN Coaching, with its emphasis on WS *IQ*, WFA, and LEAD, will point toward a wide and integrated set of opportunities for success while building the entire system's capacity to manage itself into the future.

WFA – *Whole Field Alignment*

WFA – The "WHOLE FIELD ALIGNMENT MODEL" that is shown in the following diagram is the ALIGN Coaching tool for assessing the present state of the system, imagining the desired future state and pinpointing aspects of the system for change to bring about the critical mass that is required to change a whole system.

WHOLE FIELD ALIGNMENT MODEL

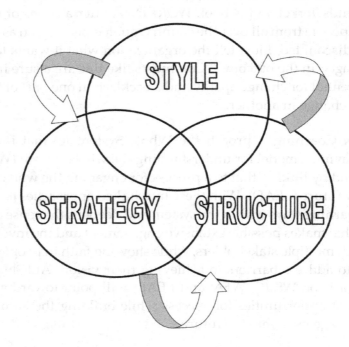

WFA is composed of the three key arenas of systems that need to be investigated in order to gain a full and complete understanding of what is really going on. The three arenas are **STYLE, STRATEGY** and **STRUCTURE.**

Since these three describe the "field" (the whole system), in my coaching I think of the investigation I (with my client) conduct into the three arenas as a "Field Inquiry." The integrated knowledge derived from a Field Inquiry allows the formulation of a comprehensive view of the entire system, laying the groundwork for our engagement.

Coaches, by expanding their co-inquiry (inquiry with the client, and often with a larger group of stakeholders) into what is occurring in the whole field, find that the essential aspects of the system become clear, making whole field change possible. The Field Inquiry into the three arenas of the field also leads to sustainable change.

A Field Inquiry: Linear vs. Whole Field Thinking

Linear (non-whole field) thinking posits that there is a root cause to any situation – just one answer to "why" and that answer needs to be dug out in order to be eliminated. Unfortunately, many people in systems like this idea of "cut to the chase" and "bottom-lining". One problem/one answer, however, is much too simple to be helpful in understanding and resolving most system issues.

Take, for a simple example, a typical car accident. Too many would jump in to say, "The driver was probably drinking," or propose some other single cause.

But research shows us that the causes of car accidents include many more factors. Perhaps a few more questions that delve into the whole field would serve to better understand why the accident occurred.

A Field Inquiry into:

STYLE: Is the driver inexperienced? Were they drinking?

STRATEGY: Were they driving too fast for road conditions? Did passengers distract them?

STRUCTURE: Did they have their seat belts buckled? Did the driver receive a phone call, or were they texting while driving?

It is the linking of these potential causes that creates the circumstances required for a car accident. Indeed, seldom can the cause of an accident, or a system misalignment for that matter, be isolated. Just like the long list of factors that can lead to an accident, there are multiple contributors to misalignment and a system's breakdowns. Each item on the list is usually insufficient in itself to lead to a breakdown; only jointly are these causes enough to create one.

As coaches we know that our assessments must consider the whole system. They must get at the true nature of the difficult situations our clients find themselves in and the opportunities that arise. It's just that many of us believe there isn't a way to capture all the data about what is going on. Sometimes it seems like a hopeless task to gather enough data to get a full picture of what influences the current situation, to get your arms around it. Whole Field Alignment was developed to respond to that challenge. Using this model, coaches will be applying a tool for whole system data collection and understanding that is simple to apply, yet comprehensive in the view of the system that results.

The LEAD Phases

LEAD, also shown in the "ALIGN COACHING" diagram, is the phased coaching process that brings about transformational change. In my work, and in that of those whom I have trained to apply LEAD, we have learned that a coach steeped in how to engage their clients in a deep change process via the application of LEAD can serve as the best-equipped guide on the road to a sustainable reformulation of the system.

The LEAD Phases

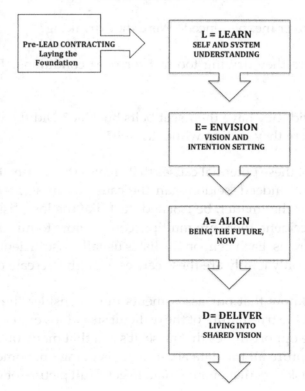

The LEAD Phases, as shown in "The LEAD Phases" diagram, is composed of four parts: Learn, Envision, Align and Deliver. Added to those is a contracting process called Pre-LEAD Contracting.

Learn involves the coach and client in a process for self and system understanding. It may include a personal inventory and stakeholder interviews covering achievements, innovations, strengths, unique gifts and talents, high point moments, internal conversations, stories – both limiting and supporting – and insights into deeper spirit.

Envision is time spent on vision and intention setting. It may include processes for identifying a client's best self, developing a meaningful and comprehensive vision story, and ensuring that the vision is fully formed and whole field (viewed through the three lenses of Style, Strategy and Structure).

Align, via the creation of Statements of Possibility, will focus the client on how to integrate the dream of the future into daily living so they can start generating aspects of that imagined future immediately.

In **Deliver,** as a coach you will work with your client to design the processes and structures that enable them to both share their vision and also continue living it. A key aspect of whole field change, the Deliver Phase is often overlooked or ignored in other coaching and consulting approaches, or coaches assume it will roll out on its own as an unstructured follow-up to what I call, "offsite euphoria". To guarantee sustained change, well-thought-out structures need to be put into place to carry the vision forward and ensure its integration into organizational life.

LEAD is a Whole Field Alignment Inquiry

As shown in the "LEAD is a WFA INQUIRY" diagram, you will work with your clients to ensure that the three inquiry arenas of WFA show up in each phase of LEAD. This is a cross check to demonstrate that the client's system would be engaged in systemic change every step of the way in your coaching engagement with them.

LEAD is a WFA INQUIRY

Applying Whole Field Alignment throughout LEAD

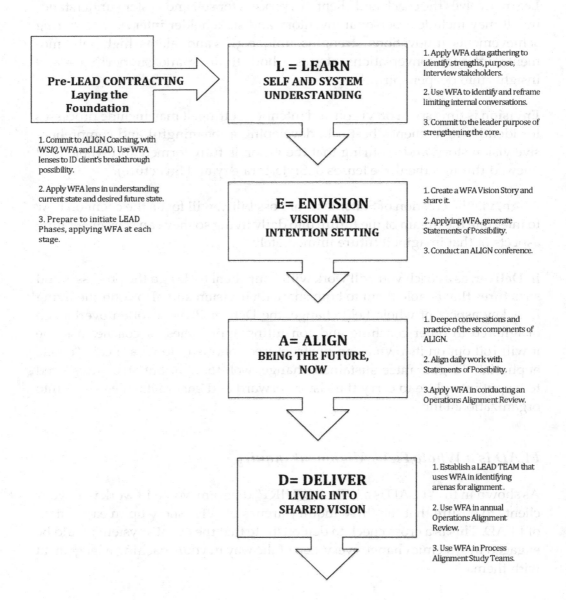

**Pre-LEAD CONTRACTING
Laying the
Foundation**

1. Commit to ALIGN Coaching, with WS*IQ*, WFA and LEAD. Use WFA lenses to ID client's breakthrough possibility.

2. Apply WFA lens in understanding current state and desired future state.

3. Prepare to initiate LEAD Phases, applying WFA at each stage.

**L = LEARN
SELF AND SYSTEM
UNDERSTANDING**

1. Apply WFA data gathering to identify strengths, purpose, Interview stakeholders.

2. Use WFA to identify and reframe limiting internal conversations.

3. Commit to the leader purpose of strengthening the core.

**E= ENVISION
VISION AND
INTENTION SETTING**

1. Create a WFA Vision Story and share it.

2. Applying WFA, generate Statements of Possibility.

3. Conduct an ALIGN conference.

**A= ALIGN
BEING THE FUTURE,
NOW**

1. Deepen conversations and practice of the six components of ALIGN.

2. Align daily work with Statements of Possibility.

3.Apply WFA in conducting an Operations Alignment Review.

**D= DELIVER
LIVING INTO
SHARED VISION**

1. Establish a LEAD TEAM that uses WFA in identifying arenas for alignment.

2. Use WFA in annual Operations Alignment Review.

3. Use WFA in Process Alignment Study Teams.

For example, in the LEARN Phase, the WFA lenses would be used in data gathering and data assessment, including making meaning of the data. Also, a more thorough understanding of your client's limiting beliefs can occur when your beliefs and values conversations with them are filtered through the Style, Strategy and Structure lenses.

In the ENVISION Phase, during which you would facilitate the client's representation of their imagined future, filtering this through the WFA lenses is an essential step toward encouraging them to design a vision that is compelling.

Finally, in DELIVER, WFA is an essential tool. The WFA lenses are used, for example, during the Operations Alignment Review for sorting and understanding all the information that needs to be presented and understood. It is also during the DELIVER Phase that what needs to be done to align daily reality with the client's vision is identified as a comprehensive WFA intervention.

Therefore, what you are seeing in the "LEAD is a WFA Inquiry" diagram is how what might appear to be a step-by-step change process, can, with attention and intention, actually be a whole system one. This necessitates applying WFA throughout the LEAD Phases in the ALIGN Coaching engagement.

ALIGN, a Coach's Guide is packed with new tools for coaches

With ALIGN Coaching you coach whole systems, not just parts. Your commitment is to assist your clients in imagining the possibilities of the future, and then bringing the hoped for and imagined future into the present. With ALIGN Coaching you are also committing to increasing your own knowledge of and capacity to apply Whole System *IQ (intelligence)*. This new level of system intelligence that you'll bring to your client engagements allows you to support your clients going through significant change – and make it sustainable. You will bring a comprehensive approach to system understanding and the capacity for enacting whole field change.

Whole Field Alignment (WFA) and LEAD are the tools that make Whole Field Inquiry possible. Putting them in your toolkit, along with **Operations Alignment Review, LEAD TEAM, and Process Alignment,** which are also introduced in *Align, a Coach's Guide,* assures you a mastery level of coaching. (NOTE: Process Alignment is NOT the same as Process Improvement, Quality Improvement or other programs that take a similar approach to 'fixing' a work process. **Process Alignment**, a whole system approach, is used when work processes that aren't aligned with the vision are uncovered.)

A **LEAD TEAM**, which is introduced in Component five of ALIGN Coaching, is a structure that has been tested in several organizations and used successfully as a means for delivering on the commitments made during earlier phases of LEAD.

John Kotter[6], in his article about what is needed to be successful in a change effort, cites the requirement for a strong and committed "guiding coalition" of internal change agents. *ALIGN, a Coach's Guide* describes the formulation of a new structure, the LEAD TEAM, which overlays without replacing the current leadership structure, and creates a whole system leadership group by including representation from each organizational level or unit. The adjunct leadership group that is formed has the job of delivering on Whole Field Alignment by extending action out over time to ensure sustained commitment to the change.

Structuring a LEAD TEAM, much like Kotter's guiding coalition, will bring input from all corners of the system. A LEAD TEAM, however, differs from the steering committee or guiding coalition in that the new structure will be added on an ongoing basis to support system governance. This structure is designed to go beyond the leadership hierarchy to expand change leadership throughout the system, plus give outside-chain-of-command members a clear mandate to touch the whole system to ensure the success and sustainability of the change effort.

Some processes may have been already poorly functioning prior to the ALIGN Coaching engagement and, in fact, if discovered in an **OPERATIONS ALIGNMENT REVIEW**, may have been one factor that led to the request for coaching in the first place. A Field Inquiry always precedes an Operations Alignment Review to assess the whole system's functioning. The LEAD TEAM may take on the role of conducting this Field Inquiry.

PROCESS ALIGNMENT may be needed where there is significant internal conflict over diverse beliefs, values, strategic intention, direction, priorities, customer requirements and/or professional opinions about what is right or wrong. Once a process, either within a team, department or workgroup, or between departments, divisions or regions, is identified as being out of sync with the envisioned style, strategy and structure of your client's system, stakeholders in that process can apply Process Alignment Tools to help them understand the whole field causes of misalignment, and ultimately to design a whole field intervention to realign the system with its vision. Training stakeholders in Process Alignment Tools is the aspect of ALIGN Coaching that is designed to prepare people in your client systems for that engagement. The LEAD TEAM members may become co-trainers, or carry on this work after a train-the-trainer session with you.

Putting it all together

Even though so integral to the success of the transformational change process, as coaches we still have lots more we can learn about aligning with vision. I see this book as increasing the knowledge base of coaches to a level that will bring about the radical shift in practice that we need to help our clients accomplish system-wide, sustainable, whole-hearted and heart-felt change.

ALIGN, a Coach's Guide **brings together the essential pieces to support this kind of coaching. This includes:**

- **ALIGN, the Six Components**

- **WS *IQ* (Whole System Intelligence)**

- **WFA (Whole Field Alignment)**

- **The LEAD Phases (Learn, Envision, Align and Deliver)**

The components of ALIGN are covered in Part One of this book. WS *IQ*, and WFA are detailed in Part Two, and LEAD is covered in Part Three.

Also, in Part Three, additional coverage of the ALIGN Phase of LEAD will extend your understanding of what's required for aligning every significant aspect of the system with your client's vision of the future.

In all three parts of *Align, a Coach's Guide,* intervention design and approaches for implementation of whole field change processes are suggested, including step-by-step instructions for a number of exercises. These may be used in one-on-one coaching sessions with your client, or in offsite meetings with other system stakeholders present.

May you find that the above listed models, guides and tools deepen the work you do with your clients – you and they deserve it.

Overview: Mastery of Coaching in Whole Systems

Masterful coaching goes beyond competence. Master coaches have a sense of purpose: coaching is their calling. They are systems thinkers, open to lifelong learning and widely read across multiple fields. They understand that mastery is not about the achievement of some designation, but rather about the journey. They also need to be scrupulously honest, especially with themselves.

As the former Department Chair and Lead Faculty of the Coaching and Consulting in Organizational Systems graduate program at LIOS College of Saybrook University, and as the developer of the International Mastery of Coaching program for The Leading Clinic, I applied a coaching competency model that resulted in aspiring coaches being fully prepared and capable of increasing the range and effectiveness of their work with their clients.

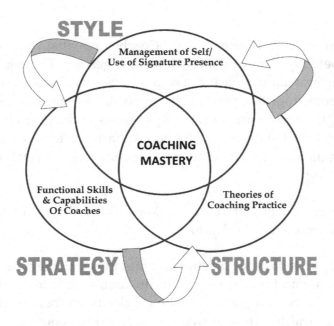

**MASTERY OF COACHING
IN WHOLE SYSTEMS**

The template of that model is pictured in the "MASTERY OF COACHING IN WHOLE SYSTEMS" diagram. It includes capacity building for coaches in three categories:

- Management of Self/Use of Signature Presence (COACHING STYLE)
- Functional Skills and Capabilities of Coaches (COACHING STRATEGIES)
- Theories of Coaching Practice (STRUCTURE OF COACHING)

Together these three components form the foundation of an ideal and complete education in whole system coaching, and, when practiced, they lead to the mastery needed for ALIGN Coaching success.

Management of Self refers to how you engage with clients in a healthy, honest relationship and includes your ability to be civil when challenged, manage conflict and ambiguity, use yourself as the source of information about what is occurring in the system, and live your values. In these aspects of self-management you serve as a model for your clients.

Your Signature Presence is the full integration of your unique personal qualities, experiences and learning in what you offer your clients – it is the way you bring every part of yourself to the client system, and what differentiates you from others.

The Functional Skills and Capabilities of Coaches are what you, as a coach, can actually competently *do* during a coaching engagement. There is a long list of skills needed to be a master coach, but some of what's included is your approach to bringing people together, your ability to positively communicate and listen for both strengths and limitations, your processes for helping clients tell their vision story, and your skills as a facilitator. A master coach's competencies can be further classified as generative, affirmative, collaborative, catalytic and whole field harmonizing.

These are described in detail in the Mastery of Coaching Checklist for Certification, found in the Addendum.

Theory is vital as the basis for practice and provides you, the coach, with lenses for understanding and intervening in individual, family, team and organizational systems. A coaching master will have clarity on their ascribed theories of how to build healthy whole systems, how to bring about systemic and sustainable change, how to stay in right relationship with clients, and how to build leadership and human capacity. Your theory of practice is the foundation of your point of view.

As a reader of this book, you have access to the potential for Mastery of Coaching

In *ALIGN, a Coach's Guide*, the three components of coaching mastery – Theories of Practice, Functional Skills and Management of Self – are extensively covered. When these are combined with your varied life experiences, and the knowledge you've drawn from them – your Signature Presence – you have the opportunity to develop excellence in your coaching – to *master* coaching.

Here is what is covered in this book in each Mastery of Coaching component:

Management of Self/Use of Signature Presence

- Values the balancing of expressing one's own position with an openness to another's point of view
- Invites inclusion and engagement
- Listens for positive intention
- "Sees" the system and is aware of induction into the field
- Practices asking for help and feedback
- Builds rapport and empathy
- Lives espoused values in everyday actions
- Prioritizes the positive while being honest and authentic

Functional Skills and Capabilities of Coaches

- Competently uses positive language and knows how to write Statements of Possibility
- "Fanning" Communication and the structures of Reframing
- Diagnosing whole systems and designing whole system change interventions
- Facilitation of operations, process and structural alignment conversations
- Facilitation of vision story-telling

- Identification of process misalignments and opportunities for alignment with vision
- Reframing of limitations into positive possibilities
- Application of well-formed conditions for vision stories
- Ability to build client's and client system's self-worth, hope and capability
- Able to align differences; able to facilitate the creation of new stories

Theories of Coaching Practice

- Systems Theory: Whole System *IQ* and Whole Field Alignment
- Theory of the sources of health in whole systems: self-worth, hope and capability
- Theory of Leaders Purpose: Leadership for a Healthy World model
- Components of ALIGN Coaching: LEAD (Learn, Envision, Align, Deliver)
- Theory of Change and sources of the predicament
- Theory of vision story-telling and the criteria for structuring for alignment with ones dream of the future
- Theory of choice as a requirement for sustainable change

So take a deep dive with me into acquiring the Theories of Coaching Practice, becoming proficient in the Skills and Capabilities of Coaching, and gaining facility in Management of Self that are presented in the following guide. These competencies will support your being a coaching master.

PART 1

ALIGN COACHING

"The most empowering condition of all is when the entire organization is aligned with its mission, and people's passions and purpose are in sync with each other."

– **Bill George**[7]

ALIGN COACHING

The juxtaposition of vision (what we want) and a clear picture of current reality (where we are relative to what we want) can generate creative tension, pulling the future into the present. This happens when the future is so compelling it calls on us to stretch ourselves towards being what we envision. This is what happens in ALIGN Coaching.

Possibilities, as we imagine them, are what bring the future to life. While traditional problem-solving concerns making improvements on the past, people and systems are drawn forward by the alluring nature of their envisioned future. This occurs when we engage our clients in creative thinking about a possibility that is so energizing it brings out in them the skills, talents and resources to make that future happen, starting now.

As we will learn in Part Three, possibilities are the bridge from the ENVISION Phase to the ALIGN Phase of LEAD. In the ENVISION Phase, the client's first draft of Whole Field Statements of Possibility will be developed. This involves translating what was imagined (seen in the mind's eye, felt and heard) when envisioning the future into a set of precise descriptions responding to the question, "What would it be like if it was happening today?"

In the ALIGN Phase, you will coach your client in completing the development of their Statements of Possibilities, creating a powerful guiding set of declarations describing the imagined future, and begin working with them to engage their systems in the actions their Statements of Possibilities describe.

Dr. Julie Connor, author of *Dreams to Action Trailblazer's Guide*, said, "Your goals and tasks either align with your dream and core values or they don't. It's that simple."[8]

In other words, clients, with your coaching, have to figure out what it will take, on a daily basis, to get from here to there. When you get there, the whole field will be aligned.

The Six Components of ALIGN Coaching

By focusing on the following six components of ALIGN, your clients will accomplish profound, whole field shifts in themselves and in their everyday work life, and begin building the critical mass needed across the systems they are in, as the tipping point to transformational change.

Component 1
FRAME THE CONVERSATION

> Change the field by engaging the whole system in a new, more constructive and optimistic conversation about itself and about others. This includes listening for understanding, deploying positive regard, reframing towards the positive, and promoting balance in the tension between attending to your relationship with others (joining) and attending to self (self-expression, differentiating).
>
> **The focus is on** intentional, open listening, reframing limiting beliefs held about self, others and the world, and seeking relational balance.
>
> **Outcome:** Allows shifting to an internal and external positive conversation that supports alignment with the vision.

Component 2
STRENGTHEN THE CORE: SELF-WORTH, HOPE and CABILITY

Asking, "What is already working and aligned?" resources clients and supports them in building a whole field with a profound sense of self-worth, hope and capability at the core.

The focus is on elevating core strengths, valuing others and self, positive intention, enabling others to engage effectively, and leading with a sense of self-worth, hope and capability.

Outcome: Develops whole field health beginning with health at the core.

Component 3
TELL YOUR VISION STORY

Embracing the story of the individual/organization towards whom/which the envisioned image points. This clarifies the path the client must take and the direction they should be heading to get stakeholders on board in living into a shared vision.

The focus is on generating a shared strategic vision story, with compelling images of the future, which allows stakeholders to cohere around the stated possibilities.

Outcome: Imagines and frames the vision story as your client prepares for sharing it and co-creating it with all stakeholders.

Component 4
GENERATE POSSIBILITY

Establish methods and channels for embedding the Vision Story into organizational life. This ensures understanding and support for its enactment as part of the system's governing structure.

The focus is on making clear, passionate and whole field Statements of Possibility that will align actions with the vision; and communicating these possibilities throughout the whole field.

Outcome: Possibilities are what bring the future to life. Problem-solving concerns making improvements on the past, but people and systems are drawn forward by the compelling nature and force of the future. The expected outcome is that the generated possibilities will become the organization's story, helping to clarify its purpose, values and aspirations.

Component 5
ALIGN OPERATIONS and ESTABLISH A LEAD TEAM

Both the OPERATIONS ALIGNMENT REVIEW PROCESS and establishing a LEAD TEAM are a means for creating aligned internal business operations. While an Operations Alignment Review generally involves the organization's designated leaders, with stakeholders providing consultation, setting up a LEAD TEAM involves establishing a cross-functional, cross-level group of employees, with representation from people at all levels of the system. These representatives are charged with the ongoing work of aligning the whole field with the system's vision.

The focus is on inclusion of employees and stakeholders in how the system works on an ongoing basis, and aligning that with the vision, using Whole Field Alignment assessment and work design tools.

Outcome: A Field Inquiry that leads to an aligned whole field, where the daily reality of the organization's stakeholders affords an ongoing experience of living their co-created vision.

Component 6
TEACH PROCESS ALIGNMENT

After completing an OPERATIONS ALIGNMENT REVIEW, and setting up a LEAD TEAM, specific processes that aren't fully aligned with the Vision Story are identified. A study team of all stakeholders in a process is formed. This study team applies PROCESS ALIGNMENT TOOLS to both a) understand what is going on that prevents a process from working, and b) recommend a process restructuring to ensure the process gets aligned.

The focus is on developing each person's ability to understand the whole field, assessing where it is not yet aligned with the vision, and recommending a system of changes where needed.

Outcome: A deepening of shared vision as teams come together to resolve misalignments in daily work processes.

Impacting Style, Strategy and Structure

Engaging in these six components is intended to set the stage for Whole Field Alignment. Each of the six is related to a whole field intervention into style, strategy and/or structure.

The six ALIGN Components in which the three arenas of Whole Field Alignment show up most clearly are:

Making change in the field's <u>Style</u>: **Components 1 & 2**

FRAME THE CONVERSATION

STRENGTHEN THE CORE: self-worth, hope and capability

Making change in the system's <u>Strategy</u>: **Components 3 & 4**

> TELL YOUR VISION STORY

> GENERATE POSSIBILITY

Making change in the system's <u>Structure</u>: **Components 5 & 6**

> ALIGN OPERATIONS and ESTABLISH A LEAD TEAM

> TEACH PROCESS ALIGNMENT

Unlike methodologies such as Lean, Continuous or Quality Improvement, and Six Sigma, which can assist only in solving problems in a work process, Whole Field Alignment supports the change by broadening understanding of the whole system and setting an expectation for behaviors that can bring forward a shared vision. By focusing on the six components of ALIGN as described above, ALIGN Coaching builds in positive consequences for new behaviors to sustain the change.

This occurs because clients and their system stakeholders are led to envision a positive whole system, and then are invited to engage in creating a productive relationship between these six components of ALIGN and their strategic vision story – a much more robust and sustainable approach to whole system change. Engaging the whole field in the components of ALIGN establishes a culture of learning, commitment, and teamwork.

"A change in action is preceded by a change in the conversation. Old conversations lead to old actions."

– Peter Block[9]

ALIGN, COMPONENT 1

FRAME THE CONVERSATION

Organizations can be described as a network of concurrent and sequential conversations that establish the frame in which people interpret the world around them.[10] Coaches help their clients become aware of this conversational network and learn how to impact it to achieve alignment with their vision. Clients will want to have the tools to generate positive internal and external conversations.

Conversations are both internal to each individual, forming their mental model, and external between people or groups, both verbal and non-verbal. Transforming the conversation to align with vision is a STYLE change (see Part Two). Because people need to feel connected to one another, here and now, in a relational system, such as an organization, they will be engaged in multiple, conversations. Of these, whole-person, positive conversations are the ones that create productive alignment.

As a coach you will want to introduce clients to the understanding that everything that's happening is a conversation, even if unspoken, because a conversation is anything that sends a message to others. For example, when a leader says they have an "open door policy", they generally are hoping to convey a message of invitation to employees to come talk over their concerns. A real *open door* occurs when the leader actually listens to the employee that comes to talk with them, as listening, a non-verbal act, is the message.

Watzlawick, Bavelas, and Jackson, communication theorists, wrote, "You cannot *not* communicate"[11] (and I add, you cannot not influence the communication network). Becoming aware of how their conversation is being interpreted, clients can raise the level of emotional engagement that employees bring to company life through conscious, deliberate and specifically focused conversations.

Leadership is a positive conversation

Leaders play a special role in setting the stage for healthy whole systems, which they do via the way they speak of and act regarding themselves and those around them. Because their choice to build a positive context for productivity and creativity at work defines them in their leadership role, we can say, "leadership *IS* a positive conversation."

The positive conversation of leaders is not talking for talk's sake. Rather, their conversations are the heart and soul of any thriving organization's culture. They are the leaders' style, as well as their strategic communications methodology incorporating very specific techniques, such as reframing towards the positive, to bring about connectivity and alignment.

However, if what leaders say and what they do initiates a negative conversation, or an incongruent one (saying one thing and doing something else), the resulting leader-employee relationship is weakened and is likely to lack commitment to a whole system change process. A simple example of this is the feeling employees have about themselves after a meeting with their leader that was filled with interruptions; they often report having the sense of "I am not valued or worthy of attention." So saying you have an open-door policy, and having it interpreted the way one hopes, are two separate conversations.

A happy birthday story

Understanding this, a newly appointed healthcare CEO in Southern California sought a way to shift the hostile culture amongst employees and between them and administration that existed in the system he came in to lead. He knew he wanted to connect with employees, and, equally important, he wanted them to connect with each other – to recognize they were part of a whole.

He began hosting a birthday party every month, open to any employee whose birthday fell in that period. This CEO sang "happy birthday" to them, cut and served the cake, and asked all the attendees what they were going to give themselves for their birthday present. After a few months of celebrating birthdays, even doctors started showing up for the cake and conversation.

To achieve the results desired in a communication requires that clients learn how to *frame* the communication. A frame is the setting within which a communication occurs. It is the context of the communication, the structure that coveys its' meaning. In the birthday party example above, the CEO communicated much more than just talking about his open door would; the birthday party, and the time devoted to it, spoke of his connection to employees and his authentic, personal interest in them. By framing the conversation in the form of the monthly birthday party, when he wished them a happy birthday, they knew he meant it.

The frame is the construct that can lead us to be attached to a belief, sometimes in a way that seems unreasonably so. Changing the frame – reframing – is a way you can shape another's belief system to achieve the conversational results you desire.

Framing with an emphasis on the positive begins in the LEARN Phase

Leaders, teams, organizations, families and communities are inspired by being seen through a positive lens. In the LEARN Phase of LEAD described in Part Three, your clients will begin to frame the conversational network of their systems, leaning away from negative language and conversations and towards the positive and the affirmative. Their language frames and transforms people around them while shaping their minds and influencing their behavior. This positive climate is achieved by purposefully eliminating or minimizing the use of negative words, by introducing and emphasizing positive words, and by reframing. Then this becomes the foundation of a *conscious culture*, what John

Mackey, co-founder of Whole Foods Market, said "allows the organization to fulfill its higher purpose."[12]

Your coaching will encourage your client to begin using positive language to describe the environment and to focus discussions on when people are at their very best. This includes highlighting the organization's achievements, strengths, values and hopes, and, particularly for an individual, what is personally meaningful to them. It includes acknowledging the contribution made by people in the past. Clients can also be coached to use powerful words such as passion, discovery, joy, inviting, exploring, generosity, hopefulness and personal breakthrough when speaking about their vision.

Tojo Thatchenkery once wrote, "By intentionally focusing on another's positive attributes, a reality different from the "problem person" is created. And in the process, the person is also transformed."[13] He believes that positive change occurs when people *decide* to commit to it, i.e., that commitment is based on choice. A person chooses to support something or someone when they believe their own contributions are valued, and when they are seen in a positive light. When this happens, people will work together to produce shared value, and not just for self-interest.

Our brains make sense of the world by framing. Framing is the way we put things into different contexts to create meaning. It is how we add to our map of reality. We use words (spoken, unspoken, internal, external) to not only represent our experience, but to *frame* our experience. Words frame our experience by bringing certain aspects of it into the foreground and leaving others in the background.

For example, the connective words "but," "and," and "even though," lead us to focus our attention on different aspects of our experiences.

If a person says, "It's sunny today *but* it will rain tomorrow," we'll focus more on the concern that it will be raining tomorrow, not the fact that it is sunny today. If someone connects the same two expressions with the word "and", for example, "It's sunny today and it will be raining tomorrow"– the two events are equally emphasized. If someone says, "It's sunny today even though it will rain tomorrow," the effect is to focus our attention more on the first statement – that it is sunny today – leaving the other in the background.

There's framing, and then there's re-framing

A great coach, through the use of language, shifts the framework of their clients' understanding, allowing them to experience their world in a completely new way. This is *reframing*.

Reframing is a process for changing the context and meaning of a situation – especially one that is a result of limiting beliefs – to create new connections in support of new, more useful meanings. It's how we change negative belief patterns into positive ones.

Beliefs provide the reinforcement that supports or inhibits particular capabilities and actions. Beliefs determine our attitudes and opinions. They relate to *why* a particular path is taken and the deeper motivations that drive people to act or persevere. This is the why we do as we do and think as we think. Motivation is what stimulates and activates how people think and what they will do in a particular situation.

Beliefs are concepts that we hold to be true. They govern the way we behave, communicate and interact with others.

In his book *Mindworks,* Gary van Warmerdam, says, "With all our intellectual smarts and education you would think that changing a belief would be easy. Except that if it were easy we would quickly change any belief that wasn't helpful, but that doesn't always happen."[14]

But what about a belief that does change quickly? What makes some beliefs easy to change and others harder?

We all have limitations due to differing physiology and what we've learned, or not, via language and conversation; this has led to a view of reality that is ours and ours alone.

Of course, our worldview is not totally different from that of others. It overlaps everyone else's – enough, at least, for us to mostly understand, connect with, and relate to each other. But beyond that, our view of the world is unique. And it's incomplete.

We can refer to our worldview as a 'map' of the world. This is a metaphor, referencing the fact that a map – a road map, contour map, or world map – can capture a sense of what it is seeking to portray, can illustrate some aspects of it, such as scaled distance, or direction. But a map is not like being in that actual place.

We respond to the world through our internal maps; our worldview is built upon these maps, rather than on any shared view of reality. It is largely our "map of the world," rather than the world itself, that forms the boundaries of our reality.

Unlike a passive road map, however, our inner maps of reality are very active. They determine the meanings we make out of life events. In fact, they determine our experience of life. Each new experience and new meaning made gets added to our map, reinforcing, modifying, and assimilating with what was already there and making the whole thing ever more complex (and the likelihood of agreement between people ever more remote).

Thus we form beliefs, and those beliefs form us.

In order to effectively reframe a conversation, your client must first recognize that holding a belief is a choice. Having more positive, life-affirming beliefs changes lives and brings wondrous opportunities forward.

For a further discussion on the formation of beliefs and how to reframe them, see the discussion on "Change" in Part Three.

What do we want to have happen in our world?

"What do we want to have happen in our world?" is a powerful question that you can ask your client who then can turn around and ask it to initiate a system-wide, positive conversation. Asking this question and participating in the subsequent discussion engages participants in creating together. In other words, by asking the question and engaging in answering it, we together are already bringing the answer – a co-created positive conversation.

Answering the question requires all of us to be leaders. We must cross boundaries and possibly yield territory, the essential ingredients of creating together.

This is a radical departure from the conversations that some clients use to try to produce results, such as commanding, exhorting, threatening, demanding, mandating, bribing, withholding information or persuading. These conversations of *control* usually create winners and losers, and fractured relationships. A co-created conversation has everyone winning. In his interview in Harvard Business Review, John Mackey said, "You have to recognize the stakeholder model: customers, employees, investors, suppliers, larger communities, and the environment are all interdependent. You operate the business in such a way that it's not a zero-sum game."[15]

Believing this, one multinational company, committed to having conversations that mattered, met every other month, for three full days to discuss its guiding principles. They did this for an entire year, thus creating a structure for living into the question, "What do we want to bring to the world?" The exponential growth the company subsequently experienced was sourced from this foundational conversation.[16]

Rules for framing the conversation

Here are some essentials for generating an aligned, whole field and authentic conversation:

1. ENGAGEMENT

Your clients don't need to have birthday parties, but they do need to create a context where everyone is engaged and where each person is clear on what they have *at stake* in the conversation.

Holding whole system, large-group gatherings to discuss important concerns such as shared vision, mission and values is one way to involve all parts of the system. Asking questions such as "What will be our legacy?" or "What are you planning to contribute today?" stimulates commitment, co-creative inquiry and learning. The client interviews with stakeholders described in Part Three, that begin in the LEARN Phase of LEAD, initiate and welcome engagement and participation.

2. CIVILITY

The word civil comes from the Latin root civilis, meaning "befitting a citizen". What this social contract, or agreement on what appropriate public behavior looks like and who deserves respect will be your client's job to establish. Civility is claiming and caring for one's identity, needs and beliefs without degrading someone else's in the process. According to the Institute for Civility in Government[17], civility is "the hard work of staying present even with those with whom we have deep-rooted and fierce disagreements."

The primary source for most conflict comes from the dynamic tension between differentiation and attunement. We want what we want (differentiation), yet we need to work with and align with others who may not want what we want (attunement). The conflict occurs between individuals taking a stand for their own point of view and not letting in the other person's voice. Civility requires both taking a position and, at the same time, acknowledging and welcoming the others position.

Civility can best be understood by thinking of it as a balance of tension, much like a coiled spring, but one that is loosely bound, allowing for movement towards and away from the other, as in the following diagram:

Differentiation ——— Attunement

Taking a stand for yourself; having your own point of view of what matters.

Listening to the other and being open to their influence; leaning in and aligning with them.

Stakeholders in the system need to know what the level of respect will be. Encouraging civility, and modeling it, becomes part of the client's work.

3. MEANINGFUL CHOICE

In order to fully embrace their ownership in the positively framed conversation of the system, there needs to be a choice to be or not be in that system, to participate or not. Stakeholders require having meaningful choice or they will take their skills and abilities elsewhere (or, as the expression goes, "they will take their marbles and go home").

Without the option of choice, being able to make conscious choices, and having the opportunity to influence the situation, participants become passive players instead of co-creators. Reframing the whole system's conversation from one of *have to* (What choice did I have?) to one of *choose to* (freedom to select from an array of options) opens the system to the new possibilities for trust, collaboration and creativity that most organizations are seeking in order to remain competitive.

Choice is the act of making a decision when faced with two or more possibilities. Your client's strategy would be to ensure there is opportunity for choice and capacity for choice, as well – and that if the choices pertain to things that matter, trust that others will choose wisely and well.

4. THE AFIRMATIVE WAY

Your clients need to attend to their verbal and non-verbal communications and commit to a minimum ratio of three to one of positive to negative expressions. This will be discussed further in Part Three.

To accomplish this, first ask your client to notice the language of their statements, announcements, phone calls, emails and letters. What is the message that is being sent? Then ask them to pay attention to how they listen, their tone of voice, and even the look on their face when they walk down the hall. What are they *saying*? Ultimately their conversation should be one of affirmation and inclusion.

Dr. David Cooperrider, developer of Appreciative Inquiry, wrote of "the affirmative basis of organizing," suggesting that systems are governed and maintained by affirmations about what they are and what they could become. He wrote,

"In many organizations that have experimented with it, people have come to believe that organization-wide affirmation of the positive future is the single most important act that a system can engage in if its real aim is to bring to fruition a new and better future."[18]

And Stephen Covey once said, ""Leadership is affirming people's worth and potential so clearly that they are inspired to see it in themselves."[19]

THE COACH'S JOB IS TO ENCOURAGE USEFUL AND POSITIVE CONVERSATIONAL FRAMING.

Coaching Checklist: Are you helping your clients . . .

☐ Find ways to include others, seeing them as adding value to the conversation?

☐ Be clear about the impact of framing the conversation and seek to remove limitations through conversational reframing?

☐ Speak with conviction about their vision story and the meaning of work?

☐ Reframe the context towards a more positive meaning?

☐ Refer to the past as the positive foundation of the present?

☐ Be conscious of having a positive conversation vs. negative (three positive to one negative statement) both internally and externally?

☐ Affirm, rather than correct others?

☐ Find a fair balance between differentiation and attunement?

"Imagine an organization full of people who come to work enthusiastically, knowing they will grow and flourish; they are intent on fulfilling the vision and goals of the larger organization."

– Charlotte Roberts[20]

ALIGN, COMPONENT 2

STRENGTHEN THE CORE: SELF-WORTH, HOPE AND CAPABILITY

The desire to engage our clients in deeper, more lasting and profound change leads to our choice of ALIGN Coaching with its focus on whole system intelligence (WS *IQ*), Whole Field Alignment and the client's development of their positive core. One of your coaching goals would therefore be to create a relationship through which clients see themselves and their systems in new, more complete and positive ways, enabling them to be more effective in building action-oriented teams to achieve a dreamed of breakthrough.

ALIGN Coaching via LEAD uses inquiry and discovery to increase the client's level of awareness and personal mastery. The belief is that your clients cause, through conversation, the climate, environment and context to empower individuals and teams, leading to their fulfillment, job satisfaction and both personal and business success. This sets the stage for having a positive impact on their communities with the hope and expectation that your clients and members of their systems will engage in actions that contribute to a better world.

John Nicholls[21] points out that a leader needs to be vitally concerned with what people are thinking and feeling and to focus on identifying strengths.

An element of the system that must be assessed is human perception: what influences perception and how perception evokes behavior.[22] Through ALIGN Coaching, the client achieves breakthroughs, however the most important breakthrough is in understanding that when they have a sense of their own self-worth, hope and capability, they can create a context for themselves and others to have this empowering sense of self. When spread throughout the system, the system and the people in it will achieve their maximum potential.

Deeply engaging your clients in this allows them to define and achieve professional and personal goals in ways that would not be possible otherwise. This is because you, their coach, actually shifts the way they *see* – particularly how they see themselves and others around them.

For nearly two decades, working with global thought-leaders and with development and change professionals from across the US and Canada, Asia and Russia, I engaged in an in-depth research process on what contributes to healthy human interaction and to positive conversations – to seeing the world in new, less limited and more open and constructive ways. Based on this investigation into high performing individuals, teams and organizations, the research team came to understand that when people have **a clear sense of their own self-worth, hope and capability**, there exists for them the potential for exceptional accomplishment.[23] Without this, it becomes easy to fall into a sense of worthlessness, hopelessness and helplessness.

From this insight, we developed **The Leadership for a Healthy World** model.

Coaching to strengths: Leadership for a Healthy World

Due to the increasing complexity of organizations and the rise of challenges that were not present in the past, the discretionary space of employees has increased. Your client's leadership focus has had to shift from dealing with time, tasks and situations to relationships and systems.[24] Richard Pascale, one of the authors of *The Reinvention Rollercoaster*[25], was quoted as saying, "Change how you define leadership, and you'll change how you run a company." We are at that tipping point where a critical mass for changing how we think about what is required for systems leadership is occurring.[26]

The intention of the Leadership for a Healthy World model is to radically shift the way we think about and define how we lead. It is no longer about a leader knowing what should be done, and then hyping people up and setting them to work on the leader's solutions, all to the drumbeat of hot competition nipping at their heels. Being a leader today is about having a *leader's purpose*, and the trust that accrues to them when they have the kind of purpose that elevates everyone around them.

Every leader's purpose needs to be to create a healthy and integrated whole field wherein each person can excel – where each person has a sense of their self-worth and capability, and retains hope for the possibility of aligning with their vision of the future. The Leadership for a Healthy World model guides ALIGN coaches in working with their clients and client systems. With this as the overarching goal, a leader is able to enroll all of the system's stakeholders in affirming and strength-based action and engagement that brings out each person's best.

Your client will do this by first paying attention to what is going well. This means noticing, for example, instances of people doing good work, being responsive to customers or treating one another with respect and civility, in order to amplify what is being done well.

For amplifying what is working, Gervais Bushe introduced the idea of 'fanning".[27] He said, "Fanning is based on the image of fanning a small fire into a roaring blaze." Your client will want to "fan" the people and activities that are aligned with their vision.

Bushe suggests framing the fanning conversation with genuine praise and blessing. While praise refers to what has happened in the past, blessing gives approval and license for positive action in the future. Beyond any spiritual meaning, blessing in the context of work may look like allocating needed resources, clarifying roles and responsibilities, or removing roadblocks to success, as examples. He also recommends asking for more of the behavior that is working, noting the antithetical belief held by many people is that asking for more was being greedy.

The research of Dr. Ryan Niemiec of the Values In Action Institute (VIA) suggests that leaders "amplify and grow the positive"[28] focusing on, for example, self-acceptance, autonomy, goal progress, passion, and resilience. He also wrote on how a sense of ones' strengths can offset the impact of negative events.

If we believe that business can be good for the world, via our coaching we can help clients embrace the idea that people really don't need to be led. Instead, they need to be affirmed and valued, invited to create a shared vision, and acknowledged for their abilities and resourcefulness.

This then would be your focus in coaching your client: to help them align with this purpose.[29] Your client, having this as their purpose, will bring greater depth to their vision story, and positive meaning to the everyday lives of stakeholders throughout their system.

The development of these strengths begins internally; it must start with your client, and it might also be said that it starts with you. As author Greg Anderson, founder of the American Wellness Project, said, "The relationships we have with the world are largely determined by the relationships we have with ourselves."[30] Or, as Tony Robbins, another well-known researcher and human developer, once said, "What we can or cannot do, what we consider possible or impossible, is rarely a function of our true abilities. It is more likely a function of our beliefs about who we are."[31]

Research[32] has shown that experiencing themselves as worthy, hopeful and capable is the critical factor that distinguishes aligned, productive, competent and flourishing people from those that aren't. Having these factors had a profound impact on every experience a leader has, affecting how capable they were at dealing with others, to what heights they aspired and ultimately what they were able to accomplish. Having a sense of self-worth, hope and capability is therefore placed at the core of the Leadership for a Healthy World model.[33]

The LEADERSHIP FOR A HEALTHY WORLD model

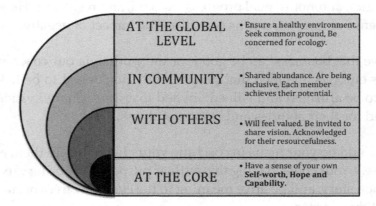

AT THE GLOBAL LEVEL	• Ensure a healthy environment. Seek common ground, Be concerned for ecology.
IN COMMUNITY	• Shared abundance. Are being inclusive. Each member achieves their potential.
WITH OTHERS	• Will feel valued. Be invited to share vision. Acknowledged for their resourcefulness.
AT THE CORE	• Have a sense of your own **Self-worth, Hope and Capability.**

LEADERSHIP FOR A HEALTHY WORLD

Here is how to understand the Leadership for a Healthy World model: AT THE CORE of leadership is the leader's purpose – what you may think of as the requirement for being a leader. It is the essential component of leadership that a person have a sense of their own self-worth, hope and capability, and an intention to bring these forward in others.

Moving out from the core, as a result of the leader's commitment to his or her own self-worth, hope and capability, WITH OTHERS, including all those directly influenced by the leader – family, in a family system, or direct reports, stakeholders, etc., in a business system – begin to experience themselves as valued, invited to work toward a shared vision and being resourceful.

People are acknowledged for their strengths, invited to celebrate accomplishments and involved in creating an environment for innovation. When people then go out and engage IN COMMUNITY, they will aspire to achieve shared economic abundance and political inclusion, creating opportunities for fully achieved potential.

AT THE GLOBAL LEVEL, the model shows how healthy communities can lead to a healthy environment, where there is a focus on seeking and finding common ground and a concern for ecology and a commitment to sustainable resourcing.

As shown in the diagram, one way to think about having a sense of self-worth, hope and capability is that it is like tossing a pebble into a pond – the impact of having this sense expands outward. We see it then touching leadership teams and all the people they lead, thus enabling individual contribution. Then, an organization's people will help transform the communities within which they live and work. And healthy communities – around the globe – create the possibility of a healthy world.

In the real world, it looks like this: via the contributions the leader and individuals in contact with the leader make, system effectiveness is impacted. From systems filled with confident, capable and hopeful people, a positive community begins to develop. And, finally, healthy, well-functioning communities contribute to global wellbeing.

This is the ripple effect that is possible when people understand their role in building personal and system-wide self-worth, hope and capability.

As authors Chunliang Al Huang and Jerry Lynch say, "By cultivating the powerful 'self' we begin to offer the possibility of change to those in our world; change comes from the individual heart and fans outward, creating a unified, interconnected community."[34] They are referring to the type of relationships between self and others, between groups and the whole that are characterized by a strong sense of heightened self-esteem, confidence, and direction.

Having a sense of self-worth, hope and capability is the antidote to feeling worthless, hopeless and helpless – the three indicators of an unhealthy mental self. Ralph Waldo Emerson, American philosopher and poet, was referring to this when he said, "Most of the shadows of this life are caused by standing in ones' own sunshine."

Self-worth, Hope and Capability

Your client and their leadership team will come to understand that when they, and other stakeholders in their system, have a sense of self-worth, hope and capability there exists for them the potential for exceptional accomplishment.

Self-Worth is the sense of one's own inherent value or worthiness as a person. It is about who you are, not about what you do; you have intrinsic value and do not have to measure yourself against others. It stems from unconditional positive regard.

Having this positive sense of self is essential for all levels of system health – individual, group or team, organization, local community and world community. Nathaniel Branden, clinician and researcher, compared the need for self-worth, to the need for calcium in the diet — if people lacked it, they didn't necessarily die, but rather became impaired in their ability to function.[35]

One of his studies at the University of Michigan found that college students who base their self-worth on external sources (including academic performance, appearance and approval from others) reported more stress, anger, academic problems and relationship conflicts. They also had higher levels of alcohol and drug use, as well as more symptoms of eating disorders. The same study found that students who based their self-worth on internal sources received higher grades and were less likely to use drugs and alcohol or to develop eating disorders.

Hope is a desire linked with positive expectations about the future. It involves optimistic thinking and focusing on good things to come. People with hope as a strength are agents of their own experience; they have the motivation and confidence that goals can be reached, and also that many effective pathways can be devised in order to get to that desired future.

Hope directs effort toward the future, and includes wishing and dreaming, aspects of the creative life that make it a joy to work towards a goal. Jerome Frank, professor of psychiatry at Johns Hopkins University Medical School, conducted research that showed how having hope was a spur to action.[36] Others who commented on the importance of hope include Peter Ericson, former VP of General Mills, who once said, "Being on the leading edge of change requires a healthy dose of hope." Reinhold Niebuhr of the Union Theological Seminary said, "Nothing worth doing can be completed in our lifetime. Therefore, we must be saved by hope."[37]

Hutson and Perry, in their book, *Putting Hope to Work*, speak of how a system that creates a vision "legitimizes hope talk."[38] The entire process of aligning with a vision story is about sharing hope – partnering in building the sense that what you are doing today will ensure you will achieve your vision of the future.

David Riddle, of Randolph Stanton Leadership Consulting, proposes that you, as a master coach, consider that your main purpose is to bring hope to a system. As a guide for his work, he uses the word hope as an acronym: H – health (providing tools for healthy conversations and relationships); O – optimism (supporting positive thinking, speaking and creativity); P – perspective (the interconnection of systems and the new views possible with reframing); E – ecology (balance and proportion in ratios that support healthy individuals, organizations and communities).[39]

He says, "For me, hope is a reverence for something unseen, but somehow experienced in my soul."[40]

Capability is simply the ability to do something. However, in the Leadership for a Healthy World model, capability refers to the confidence one has in ones' ability to cope with the basic challenges of life, including being effective at work. Words such as "expertise," "mastery," "aptitude," "fitness," and "genius" are associated with the idea of capability. We think of a capable person as skillful, creative and original.

Jim Kouses and Barry Posner's research[41] found that exemplary leaders made others feel capable, and when they did, extraordinary things got done. In their book *The Leadership Challenge*, they refer to this as "enabling others to act."

Self-worth, hope and capability are positive qualities that are intimately linked. Hope, for example, is considered the product of both *agency thinking* and *pathways thinking*. In other words, it involves perceptions that one is capable of acting effectively (agency thinking, or "I can do it") and that one also has the capability of strategizing to complete the action (pathways thinking, or "I know a way to do it"). Self-worth is a person's belief that they are worthy because they have the capacity to achieve their goal.[42]

A Story of Rabbi Levi Yitzchak of Berditchev

The Talmud, a holy book for the Jewish people, calls for everyone to be weighed "on the scales of merit", intentionally focusing on what is most pure in each person and to see their highest and holiest potential.

In the nineteenth century, a great mystic, the Rabbi of Berditchev, Rabbi Levi Yitzchak, who established the famed Chassidic Court, where thousands of his followers throughout Eastern Europe would flock to his synagogue for inspiration and guidance, was known throughout Europe as the *Master of the Good Eye*. He is remembered for his compassion and gentleness, and for his legendary love for everyone, no matter their spiritual or material state. It was said that he could see nothing of people's sins, only their virtues.

He'd roust the local drunk from his stupor on the High Holy Days, seat him at the head of the table, and respectfully ask for his wisdom.

One Sabbath, Rabbi Yitzchak met a man smoking in the street. The rabbi asked the young man if he'd forgotten that such an act is forbidden on the Sabbath. The young man replied that no, he hadn't forgotten. R. Levi Yitzchak then asked if there was some circumstance causing him to sin. The young man replied that no, he was knowingly and voluntarily sinning. Rabbi Yitzchak looked up to the sky and said, "Lord of the Universe, see the holiness of your people! They'd rather declare themselves sinners than utter a lie!"

He extended his caring to all, whether powerful or impoverished, scholarly or simple, righteous or reprobate. He brought a sense of self-worth, hope and capability to each encounter.

From his story we learn about some of the leader actions that grow whole system health:

- Don't discard people; retrain them and invite their creativity.
- Ensure learning opportunities.

- Hold conversations of valuation, not evaluation.
- Reframe. Focus on the positive intention rather than on the action itself.
- Leave the door open for people to surprise you.

Like other leaders who recognize that their purpose is to promote self-worth, hope and capability in themselves and others, John Mackey, of Whole Foods Markets, reminds us that a great work community is like any other community in how people within it can "aspire to the highest values that have inspired humans throughout time." From his experience running one of the most successful food operations of all time while seeking to live his leadership purpose on a daily basis, Mackey said he'd characterize his leadership aspiration as, "heroic, meaning changing and improving the world and standing up for what you believe is true and right and good."[43]

THE COACH'S JOB IS TO ENSURE THEIR CLIENT'S COMMITMENT TO WHOLE SYSTEM HEALTH AND WELL-BEING. FIRST THEY MUST COMMIT TO THEIR OWN.

Coaching Checklist: Are you helping your clients . . .

☐ Understand that building self-worth, hope and capability could be considered the most significant human development opportunity of this century?

☐ Build self-worth, hope and capability, which has been linked to

- diminished system stress
- improved coping
- less friction
- less conflict?

☐ Increase the team or individual's sense of self-worth, hope and capability to propel new sources of innovation, collaborative capacity and entrepreneurship?

☐ Grow the system's positive core, the source of potential flourishing at all levels of system? Health and well-being, the quality of relationships, and stakeholder motivation and performance, are impacted by their sense of self-worth, hope and capability, as is their capacity for growth and resilience supporting positive transformational change.

☐ Speak highly of others? Acknowledge their positive intention?

☐ Acknowledge the contributions and expertise of others?

☐ Give elbow-room for learning and growth?

☐ Wear the hat of hope?

☐ Be willing for people to surprise them?

"Give to us clear vision that we may know where to stand and what to stand for, because unless we stand for something we will fall for anything."

– Peter Marshall[44]

ALIGN, COMPONENT 3

TELL YOUR VISION STORY

In 1982, in the face of falling snow and freezing temperatures, Don Bennett climbed Mount Rainier, on one leg. When he was asked, ""How did you do it? How did you make it to the top of Mount Rainier on one leg?" He answered, "One hop at a time."

This is often how vision is achieved. But without it, would even one hop have been taken?

Standing at the Brandenburg Gate in West Berlin, Germany on June 12, 1987, Ronald Reagan said, "If you seek peace, if you seek prosperity for the Soviet Union and Eastern Europe, if you seek liberalization: Come here to this gate! Mr. Gorbachev. Open this gate! Mr. Gorbachev, tear down this wall!"

He was speaking of the Berlin Wall, separating East and West Berlin for more than a quarter of a century, which divided the city in half, keeping friend from friend and family members from one another. After President Reagan's declaration, the Wall came down just two years later. After twenty-five years of stasis, it took only two to achieve his vision.

As you can see from these examples, conversation about one's vision needs to come from a different place than ordinary talk. This kind of communication is called a 'stand' or a 'committed stand.' When you take a stand you have a different relationship to the circumstances — one that is not impacted by history or even reality.

Have you ever had something work no matter what the odds were? It's surprising, isn't it?

I had a recent experience of this. After dragging my feet and saying I didn't want to move from our island paradise, I realized that the huge efforts my husband and I were making to maintain our steep hillside home were ruining our physical health and negatively affecting our mental well-being, and dangerously so.

We met with a realtor friend and declared our intention to sell our home and move … wherever we would land. At the time we didn't have anything lined up, not even a rental, not even a storage unit for our 25 years of treasured possessions. Within a few weeks, however we found a place we both really liked, put in an offer, and started the packing that would lead to our moving out to a new home within a month.

This is the power of taking a stand.

I found that having a dream and speaking of it with certainty compels action. It becomes your vision story.

'Normal' conversation, filled with opinions, assessments, stories and explanations, will not bring forward the kind of action that is needed to achieve a powerful, new future. The basis for the compelling nature of a vision is that you say so. It draws power from your commitment, your word.

Declaration is the language of vision and breakthrough. A breakthrough declaration is a stand you take about the future, and about your potential to achieve something that is outside the bounds of what seems possible within current reality.

Some other examples of powerful declarations include marriage or partnership vows, and the great American declarations, including the Declaration of Independence, the Emancipation Proclamation, and John Kennedy's often quoted, "We will put a man on the moon in this decade."[45] This was first spoken in a speech Kennedy made at Rice University in September 1962. The Apollo moon landing occurred just seven years later, in July 1969, even though there had never even been a space-walk, a docking in space, no TANG created to drink, and no lunar modules had yet been built when Kennedy first shared his vision.

Declarations begin with phrases such as "I declare," "I commit to," "We will", "I am", or as Kennedy said, "We *choose* (to go to the moon)."

During LEAD, we ask our clients to declare their vision in the form of Statements of Possibility (see below in Align, Component 4 for more on Statements of Possibility), and make them systemic by including references to what they experience in all senses and see occurring in the arenas of style, strategy and structure. This ensures that their vision is robust, rich, even intense, and that it incorporates aspects of the whole field. Doing this, they are articulating their stand for a causal relationship between their everyday life and their intention for the future. Statements of Possibility are a description of what today would be like if the future was happening now; they connect the image of the future with suggested actions for today. The client then gets to live "as if" their future is happening now. Until it is.

And as author Brian Doyle once said, your clients might then "catch a story that's big enough to change the world." He also said, "Some stories are so important, so powerful, they are food."[46]

In fact, the guidance and compelling nature of declared Possibilities can be thought of as highlighting the purpose of everyday life: acting moment by moment as if one's vision is playing out exactly as one imagined it would, engaging all whom you imagine need to participate to make it so. Kennedy understood this and included in his famous "Moon Speech", the one declaring the intent to go to the moon, that doing so would "serve to organize and measure the best of our energies and skills."[47]

The declared vision story must describe a realistic and attractive future, one that is better in important ways than what currently exists. This is why a client saying they want to be "the best", or "the biggest", is not adequate or compelling. They aren't utilizing language that sets them apart. It also doesn't invite others to co-create that vision so it can become a reality. As Peter Senge said, "Few if any forces in human affairs are as powerful as a shared vision."[48] A declared and shared vision story beckons.

A vision with a story

There is an important distinction, however, between a vision *statement* and a vision *story*. Traditional vision statements can often be characterized by the overuse of similar sets of words that are not descriptive, and, let's admit it, often quite vague and dull, and filled with buzzwords and clichés. Strings of well-worn words such as "Be the number one in our field," or "To be the best … (fill in the blanks)," for example, have so little clarity and almost no detail that they say nothing about any real aspiration to an imagined future. Many of these vision statements can be substituted for someone else's. So, rather than stimulating the effort to align with and live that vision, they tend to dull energies and enthusiasm needed for integrating vision into everyday life.

Instead of being a mere cookie cutter vision statement, a deeper version of vision will connect people and, as Ira Levin wrote in *Vision Revisited*, "serve as a beacon of inspiration during times of change and disruption."[49] He suggests our coaching shift clients away from "fuzzy," and easily misunderstood vision statements towards the more descriptive and compelling vision story because the vision story produces a virtual, even *vicarious* experience of the future. This "helps people personalize it and assimilate the learning of new behaviors and performance expectations." [50]

A vision story should be written in narrative form, in the present tense, describe who is present and chronicle what specifically is happening in the imagined future as if it were happening now. With its vivid images of behaviors, environment, interactions and whole field description, this story is what will ultimately create shared meaning, and enable people to feel they can be a part of it. It will describe what life in the future would be like in a way that stakeholders can imagine themselves right there.

An important factor in creating a vision story is not to talk about concepts such as 'teamwork' or 'communication,' but rather to provide specific examples of what behaviors are occurring that might demonstrate these concepts in action.

Stories bring the future to life. Levin cites Erickson and Rossi 's research where they discovered that stories suspend everyday frames of reference, creating "trance states in listeners during which they are open to consideration of new possibilities and learning."[51]

Working with a timeframe that is three to five years out will stretch the imagination. Creating a vision story, however, is not a one-time conversation. Bringing the system in alignment with the vision story will continue via the use of Statements of Possibility, holding an Operations Alignment Review and Process Alignment. To continue to support alignment, your client will want to re-examine, update and treat the story as a work in progress.

One Agency's Vision Story

Here is an example of a vision story created by an agency I coached that was seeking to build on its success:

Our Vision Story

(Strategy)
We have talked it through and have a clear mission; we know what our purpose is. We also have agreed upon current breakthrough goals and objectives, aligned with our mission and purpose.

We are optimistic and engage with others in positive conversations about what is possible for them and for us. Through our committed intentional connections with our broader community, we are able to achieve our goals.

Our team has an unstoppable work ethic; we strive to bring our best into every interaction. We spend time strategically connecting and developing alliances and partnerships that bring win-win results for all parties involved. People in the community know our name, know our work, and know the 5-Star results we get for our clients.

(Structure)
We act as a team in taking bold action every day in pursuit of our mission. We are disciplined and demonstrate excellence in our work and in our relationships with each other. We are flexible when it comes to getting the job done; we believe we are in it together.

We are in agreement about the size, structure, and positioning of our company within the industry. Our growth is both measured and manageable. We know when "enough is enough. The people who work here are hired because they share a desire to grow personally and professionally. Team members and partners are selected based on their positive intentions for others, professional competence, personal integrity, and business results.

(Style)
We engage in deep and authentic ways with our donors, venders, clients, and their families. We tell the truth and are honest in our dealings. We delight in dialoging with stakeholders and invite them on a regular basis to co-create and update our vision story.

Our leaders thoughtfully delegate, teach, mentor, and provide encouragement and acknowledgement. Employees feel enriched by their relationships with their managers.

We are master communicators skillful in influencing and reading people. We listen generously with patience, sincere curiosity and openness to learn. We reframe limitations into positive opportunities that will benefit all parties. Everyone who comes in contact with us is made to feel significant, valued and appreciated not in spite of their differences, but because of them. We accept the polarities and paradoxes in ourselves and others. We are committed to breaking unhealthy, results-limiting patterns.

We yearn to make the world a better place to be. We start by making our homes healthier places in which to live, our workplace a more nurturing place to do our work, and our communities a supportive resource for all our neighbors.

The Vision Story for an Engineering Company

Here is an example of a vision story created by a group of engineers during a retreat as they imagined their future:

Vision 2020

We are the go-to firm in our markets, known for quality design, customer service and creativity. We are sought after by clients and potential employees. Skilled and talented staff from all walks of life want to work here. We recruit and retain diverse employees and mentor each other to our highest potential.

We have strong client relationships, built on our culture of dependability, efficiency, innovation, integrity and responsiveness – our customers keep coming back!

We are a well-organized, smoothly operating company with offices in three cities. Each year we earn certificates for employee satisfaction and corporate responsibility.

We live our values of community, integrity and effectiveness. We engage with respect, teamwork, commitment, positive relationships and fun. You can count on us to do the right thing and listen to you. We are proactive, flexible, nimble, and clear-speaking. We care for each person's life, health, and wellbeing and are a supportive and welcoming family where we can enjoy a healthy work-life balance.[52]

The mind's eye

A vision distinguishes the individual and the organization, setting them apart. Part of that is because a true vision is something you can see "in your mind's eye".

The mind's eye is the mental faculty of conceiving imaginary or recollected stories, pictured in the mind. We have, in effect, a mental whiteboard that can be watched by a mental eye. The eye is our perceptual system, our awareness. We cannot only put incoming sensory data on the whiteboard, we can also write on it mentally, and then use the same perceptual system that looks at the outside world to look at what we wrote on the board. Our brain "writes" on the whiteboard by activating some of the brain's neurons.

Your imagination has two parts. One can reform any existing pictures in the mind into a new stream at your choice. The other part is original imagination. You, in your mind, form the images per your intention. In one workshop warm-up I use, I ask participants to imagine rolling all of their concerns into a ball and placing that ball under their chair. Most people can do this. Their ball, however, might, in their mind's eye, look like something from their memory, or they might choose to create it as an original ball, with no relationship to any other with which they are familiar. If one person's ball has purple stripes and green dots and another's has holes like in a whiffle ball it doesn't change the ability to participate in the exercise. In any case one person's ball is not going to be like another's.

Each of our minds contains multiple channels of perception. We are familiar with sight, sound, touch, taste and smell, but many more channels occur such as time, emotion, location, imagination, reality, the emotional level of others, pain and unconsciousness, and one's perception of one's level of consciousness. Even one's awareness of awareness is perceived. Therefore, not only must your vision be expressed using the language of the senses, it must also beckon with other perception.

A checklist for a well-formed vision story

A well-formed vision story

- ☐ Is made and imagined by those who are enthusiastic about living it

- ☐ Is told in present tense

- ☐ Is filled with details drawn from sensory information 'seen' in the mind's eye

- ☐ Is personally meaningful

- ☐ Expresses your values and ideals

- ☐ Can be shared with members of one's system

- ☐ Describes what is happening: who is there, what you and they are doing; and what you are feeling

The Golden Circle: a guided imaging vision process

Here is a guided imaging exercise that I have used with my clients and client teams to begin the process of bringing the energy of their vision of the future into the present.

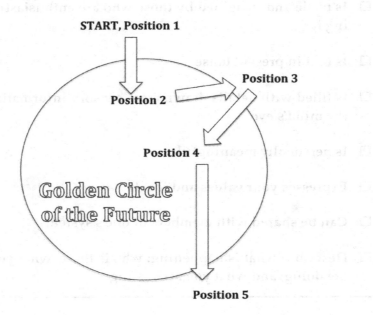

The Golden Circle [53]

Part 1. Ask your client/participants, "Thinking about your vision, "What would be a breakthrough for you?"

Have them write down what their breakthrough would be. A few words or expressions to capture the idea would be enough.

Part 2. Have your client/participants stand. Tell them that they will lay claim to this breakthrough. Say:

START (POSITION 1)

"Close your eyes and imagine that a shiny, golden circle is in front of you on the floor. This is the future when your declared breakthrough has already been achieved.

Step into the circle (POSITION 2). Notice that you are now at this time, and that you have already achieved your breakthrough. Where are you? Notice what is going on around you, see what you see and hear what you hear, what you smell and what you taste. How are you communicating and interacting with others? What is your positive intention? What is your relationship to those around you and what is it that allows for you to be so successful?

Notice how alive, positive and resourceful you are feeling. Let your mind imagine all the possibilities.

Now stand in a way that shows you have achieved your breakthrough. (Pause) Think of a gesture of resourcefulness that will serve as your private anchor to this experience and who you are; in other words, when you make this gesture you will immediately feel the resourcefulness that comes with having achieved your breakthrough.

Keeping your eyes closed, make this gesture now, as you are experiencing yourself fully competent, engaged and resourceful, having achieved your breakthrough.

Still keeping eyes closed, **step to the side and out of the circle (POSITION 3),** leaving the future there.

Now, remembering that time in the golden circle future when you have achieved your breakthrough, and the resources you have then and now, think of something you will need to do in the very near future to forward your breakthrough commitment, when you will need those resources. Imagine experiencing this situation, feeling yourself in your own body, looking through your own eyes, seeing what you see, feeling what you feel and hearing what you hear.

As you are experiencing this, **take a step back into your golden circle (POSITION 4).** Make the gesture signifying your breakthrough, and experience yourself having those feelings and resources now. Notice how you are feeling even more powerful and capable now, with your sense of already having achieved your breakthrough result.

Now **step out of the circle (POSITION 5)** and open your eyes."

Part 3. Say: "Declarations are powerful conversations for possibility. By taking a stand for your commitment in front of others, you invite their active support and the coaching you will need to accomplish your breakthrough."

Part 4. Then say, "Experiencing yourself fully congruent with your break-through possibility, make the gesture you created earlier, and declare your breakthrough vision, using the language of the declaration. (I commit to … I am …)."

Part 5. Say, "The guiding image of the future exists deep within ones internal dialogue and that of a group. Using the language of declaration begins the process of shifting the internal conversation towards anticipation of a breakthrough in results and can also release collective aspiration. This is why your having a vision is as important as is sharing it."

THE COACH'S JOB IS TO SUPPORT THE CLIENT AS THEY SEEK TO CLARIFY THEIR VISION AND FIND MULTIPLE WAYS TO SHARE IT WITH SYSTEM STAKEHOLDERS.

Coaching Checklist: Are you helping your clients . . .

☐ Ensure their vision story is well-formed, describing a compelling image of the future that they feel drawn to?

☐ Plan how to share their vision story with all their stakeholders?

☐ Co-create their vision story?

☐ Listen for possibility and become a cheerleader for it?

☐ Appeal to others to share the dream of the future?

☐ Show others how their interests and dreams can be realized?

"A vivid imagination compels the whole body to obey it."

– Aristotle

ALIGN, COMPONENT 4

GENERATE POSSIBILITY

It's time to talk about magic.

One of the definitions of magic is that it's an extraordinary power or influence seemingly from a supernatural source. In some forms of magic the magician transforms something from one state into another—a silk handkerchief changes color, a lady disappears, an indifferent card changes to the spectator's chosen card.

In our work as coaches, this is what happens: When you coach your clients to declare their vision in the form of a *Statement of Possibility*, it seems like a new present opens up that was not possible before they imagined it and spoke about it. Just like magic, it becomes so because they say so or believe it is so. The imagined future that they declared begins to unfold in the present in ways not previously thought of.

Elizabeth Gilbert in her book, *Big Magic*, says that it is "a mighty act of human love to remind somebody that they can accomplish things by themselves." She also believes we are all "walking repositories of buried treasure."[54] Generating a new possibility is that treasure.

So as we are change agents engaged in the loving and sacred conversations of coaching, we are also magicians – or magician-reminders as Gilbert might say – on an imaginative treasure hunt with our clients to clarify the possibilities that will transform today. And it turns out that our magic wand is the Statement of Possibility.

A Statement of Possibility is a clear and passionate expression of something that has the potential to occur in reality, but has not yet been manifested.

When you coach your client to declare a never-before experienced reality in the form of a Statement of Possibility, it refers to something they have likely invented and seen in their mind's eye. You have helped them to become immersed in this possibility – in the sounds and feelings of it. You may have even encouraged them to smell it and taste it.

This personal, full-bodied experience of their vision is the creative act – your client's original work of art – and just by having had this vision, they already begin bringing it forward into their lives.

Because they say so, the change begins. But it is like a long row of dominoes. Tilting the first domino will cause it to fall against the next … but only if they are aligned! Not being in alignment stops the momentum. The same is true of change. If you coach your client into alignment with their vision, everyday reality will be strongly influenced to increasingly resemble their imagined reality.[55]

Then your client will merely need to think of themselves as stepping into their creation, allowing themselves to become energized by it and initiating new everyday actions so that a match-up of every-day and imagined realities emerges.

David Cooperrider wrote, "Much like a movie projection on a screen, human systems are forever projecting ahead of themselves a horizon of expectation that brings the future powerfully into the present as a causal agent."[56] So just think of the athletes you may have heard of that imagine their ball going into the cup or across the net, if your client can imagine it, with your coaching, they will become it. Not so different than waving a magic wand!

As Willis Harman said in his book *Global Mind Change*, "By deliberately changing their internal image of reality, people can change the world."[57]

Creative images of a future possibility ensure a sense of self-worth by strengthening the capacity to recall the positive aspects of the past and to see how
strengths are manifesting in the present. They summon confident and energized action.

David Cooperrider also proposed the Simultaneity Principle: Inquiry and
change are not separate, but rather simultaneous events. This is his idea of
what accounts for how there often is no gap between imagining and realizing
ones vision.

A declared Statement of Possibility bridges the present and the future. As an
ALIGN coach, however, you may want to do some preliminary work with your
clients to help them get complete with their past. This isn't about forgetting their
past but rather diminishing or eliminating any negative impact it may have on
the present. They will "come to terms" with it, as the expression goes.

When the past no longer drives the present, there's more room for the future to
show up. Therefore, the question to ask your clients is, "Do you want the past
to create your present, or the future?

This doesn't mean that any less effort should be directed towards developing
the Statements of Possibility. Developing them engages the client in:

1. Imagining a future dream as if it were occurring now. This would be
   a future that moves and inspires, and that excites and compels fully
   committed action.

2. Speaking and sharing that image of the future, using positive, present
   tense and passionately spoken statements.

3. Utilizing the resulting description to bring about "creative tension"
   between the future and present.

The sacred and magical nature of the coaching conversation: a story about a Stewartia

Although I had had extensive training in Neuro-linguistic programming (NLP) early in my career, I had stuck to applying my learning to the business context in which I worked. I incorporated my knowledge into many of the programs I developed on communications, improving relationships, positive intention, learning strategies, sensory acuity, teambuilding and leadership, to name a few.

I steered away, perhaps unconsciously so, from other applications of NLP, such as physical healing, therapy, personal growth and belief system change. That is, until we moved to Vashon Island.

I'm not entirely sure who gave away the information on my background, but one day, out of the blue, I received a call from Jake. He told me he had cancer, and he asked me to work with him on healing using an NLP approach.

Well, to be honest, I wasn't sure what to do. I didn't want to oversell my skills or experience, but I just couldn't say no to his urgent request.

We started meeting bi-weekly, and did so for over a year. We applied some of the most powerful Neuro-Linguistic Programming change processes, many developed by Robert Dilts, my own teacher. I felt, however, that I was 'just-in-time' in my own learning. I often felt unsure of myself, and worried that I wasn't being helpful. I didn't want to be someone that gave direction, when I myself felt lost.

Jake was a young man, somewhat spiritual, who ran a retreat center with his wife, Janice. He was into healthy eating and being outdoors. In our time together, he stated that our conversations and exercises led him to a new level of wisdom and awareness, to his having many breakthroughs and insights (as did I working along with him) and, importantly, to his being able to finally speak honestly with his wife.

Did he overcome his cancer? No, he didn't.

But during this sacred time together he reported on the healing conversations he'd had with Janice, and his growing sense of self and clarity about what was his to do in the world, even as he struggled with his cancer diagnosis. He attributed much of this shift in himself to our work together, and spoke of how he was grateful now for every day of his life.

In the spirit of that gratitude, he gifted me with a somewhat rare Stewartia Tree, then only a few feet tall.

A graceful tree of many charms, Stewartia pseudocamellia (Korean or Japanese Stewartia) is known in Japan as the summer camellia, natsu–tsubaki. We planted it in a spot on our meditation path where you couldn't miss seeing and admiring it, right next to the area dedicated to Kuan Yin, Buddhist goddess of compassion.

It was beautiful, healthy and it grew. For me, it represented the magician-coach in me that was there even when I didn't know it.

During the past month, we moved from our Vashon home of 25 years. One of the saddest things about that leave-taking was that I wasn't able to take Jake's tree, now about 25 feet tall, with me. How would I remember that amazing time working with Jake, a time when I learned that my work as a coach is both sacred *and* magical?

But the final chapter of this story is that shortly after we arrived at our new home here on Camano Island, I discovered that a Stewartia Tree, big and beautiful, was growing right outside the front window!

Not as big as the one on Vashon, but blooming, blooming, blooming.

Change the way you talk about it

Some time ago, Richard Bandler and John Grinder wrote a pair of books entitled "The Structure of Magic, I and II.[58] In them, the authors shared insights from their study of grammar, and applied their discoveries to understanding and evaluating the therapeutic interventions of therapist such as Fritz Perls, Virginia Satir and Milton Erickson. In Perls', Satir's and Erickson's therapeutic interventions their clients seemed to quickly make profound and lasting change. Their work had what the authors called 'magical potency,' and Bandler and Grinder wondered why.

They asked the question, "How specifically does change happen?"

Being aware that change was taking place was one thing; understanding the specific elements that made change possible was another thing altogether. They wanted to make explicit the structure that was implicit in the amazing change accomplished by these therapists and others like them.

In Bandler and Grinder's work, linguistic analysis became the means for understanding the barriers to change that were being communicated and, at the same time, the tool for bringing about positive change. They understood that people asked for help when they were experiencing a lack of choice, and that lack of choice was expressed in the way language was used to describe a set of beliefs.

It is through understanding the structure of your client's expressions of beliefs about the world that you, as a coach, can effectively restructure a limiting belief and expand their possibilities. Changing the way they speak about something will expand their world. Merely by languaging a new possibility you are opening your client to new experiences that weren't previously in their model of what their world was like.

This calls upon us as coaches to be committed to doing work that brings forth the highest and best self that we can be, in order to bring that forth in our clients. Their world will be new as a result of this deep trust.

This is sacred work.

It is also magic.

For more on how to write Statements of Possibility see Part Three, in the section on the ENVISION Phase.

THE COACH'S JOB IS TO RECOGNIZE THAT SPEAKING ABOUT CHANGE AND THE CHANGE ITSELF OCCUR SIMULTANEOUSLY, LIKE MAGIC.

Coaching Checklist: Are you helping your clients . . .

☐ Imagine the future as if it were happening now?

☐ Use passionate language when speaking of their dream?

☐ Articulate clear and compelling Statements of Possibility?

☐ Become aware that change is happening as they speak of it?

☐ Allow themselves to become energized and transformed by their vision story and the Statements of Possibility they created?

☐ Create Statements of Possibility that open them to new choices and new experiences?

"You reinvent yourself every day. But you also get to decide every day if you are going to go forward or backward."

— James Altucher[59]

ALIGN, COMPONENT 5

ALIGN OPERATIONS AND ESTABLISH A LEAD TEAM

Misalignment between their desired future and current day-to-day operations doesn't occur because people don't care about their work or lack the desire to work hard to accomplish goals. Misalignment occurs because most of your clients' processes and procedures were designed prior to attaining clarity on their whole field vision story. The Style, Strategy and Structure of their vision story was not then expressed in Statements of Possibility, so operations weren't yet aligned, cohesive and integrated. Plus, this lack of clarity resulted in confusion regarding accountabilities and responsibilities for making operations work.

Alignment is driven by the involvement of leaders, managers and staff in developing and maintaining a culture committed to inquiry, participation, responsibility, partnership and customer satisfaction. It requires training in tools for the evaluation and alignment of processes, and the building of generative, affirmative, collaborative, catalytic and harmonizing competence that allows for maximum flexibility in adapting to changing environments and evolving customer/community expectations.

When you and your client began the ALIGN Coaching engagement you initiated with them a journey of transformation. This journey called for an inquiry identifying personal and organizational strengths and the sources of your client's vitality – an inquiry that resulted in a shift in the conversations they had been having about who they were and what was possible for them to become. The breakthrough that was articulated in your ALIGN Coaching sessions with them was a demonstration of this fresh perspective your clients can have, experiencing themselves anew and imagining a wildly successful future.

ALIGN Coaching, via the LEAD Phases, has served to allow clients to imagine reinventing themselves and their organizations, as they have courageously chosen to confront their own perceived limits and limiting points of view. They have extended their capabilities in order to achieve their vision of the future.

Your coaching helps your clients to leave behind limitations from their past so they can move forward. One of the outcomes of this coaching is for clients to be prepared for transformation, that is, to be, as the proverbial transformation of the caterpillar to a butterfly, "not more caterpillar, or a better or improved caterpillar, but a different creature altogether."[60]

In today's work environment, it is not enough just to improve. A more fundamental shift in capabilities is needed. Tracy Goss, Richard Pascale and Anthony Athos in their article, "The Reinvention Rollercoaster: risking the present for a powerful future," say that "Reinvention is not changing what is; it's creating what isn't."

The authors also state that for an organization to "reinvent itself, it must alter the underlying assumptions on which its decisions and actions are based." This, in a sense, has been one of the deeper purposes for your coaching engagement with your client – it becomes the driving reason to engage in one of two types of approaches to whole field alignment.

Two whole field methods used to match vision with day-to-day work processes

Both ALIGNING OPERATIONS, beginning with an Operations Alignment Review, and ESTABLISHING A LEAD TEAM are actions that can be taken for creating aligned internal business structures. While an Operations Alignment Review generally involves the organization's designated leaders, consulting in a multitude of ways with stakeholders, LEAD TEAM ACTION involves a cross-functional, cross-level representation from people at all levels of the system charged with aligning the whole field with their system's vision story.

An Operations Alignment Review occurs after a Field Inquiry is conducted, and is an in-depth look at the big picture as well as approaches to daily work. It addresses style issues such as communication, decision-making and leadership style; strategy issues such as marketing approaches and profitability sources; and structure issues such as operating procedures, staffing and team success indicators; and other factors that affect a business, while looking to find what might be making it unstable and misaligned with your client's vision story.

An Operations Alignment Review

It is important to any organization, whether nonprofit or for-profit, that its operations and its operational structure support its mission, values, and strategic objectives, and that its financial reporting structure mirror reality while aligning with the vision.

Financial reporting has to parallel and report on what is happening so that leaders, managers and boards have a clear understanding of the resources it takes to provide a specific service or program to further an organization's mission.

There are two parts to an Operations Alignment Review, each addressing one of the following questions:

- Is the entity organized in the optimal manner to support its mission, values and positive possibilities?

- Are day-to-day processes working smoothly and aligned with the vision?

In an Operations Alignment Review, the following actions are taken.

1. **Review of the budget to ensure that it is allocated to allow for accomplishment of the vision and mission.**

Questions: Are financial and other resources budgeted sufficiently to support accomplishing the vision and mission? Does the budget need to be revised to reflect new priorities and possibilities?

2. **Comparison of the organization's vision story and the organization chart.**

Questions: Is there congruence? Should the org chart be modified or structured with different positions than there are now? Additions? Reassignments?

3. **Determination of the organization's structure: vertical, horizontal, a loose affiliation of semiautonomous units, a hub and spoke, front office/back office or something else altogether.**

Questions: Is this the best structure to support achieving the mission, values and vision?

4. **Update role assignments and descriptions.**

Questions: Are roles clear? Will people be taking on new roles within a new structure? If so, utilize role descriptions prepared in advance.

5. **Specific arenas (specific processes) where misalignment is occurring are identified, and Process Study Teams (see Process Alignment, component 6) are chartered to align the processes with vision.**

Questions: Why is misalignment occurring? Are the right people in place to perform the necessary tasks? Are sufficient resources available? Is this a case where neither the executive nor the board of directors understands the delivery challenges involved?

Some questions related to identifying which processes are misaligned or have breakdowns:

- Are there redundant tasks between units that can be eliminated?
- Are there tasks performed in one unit that could be better performed in another?
- Are some units overloaded while others are not sufficiently tasked?
- Should some tasks be allocated more resources?
- Should managers pay more attention in some areas?
- Does information flow between units to optimize performance?

To get answers to the above questions, the Field Inquiry may employ pre-session interviews with key outside influencers such as customers/users. Talking with major suppliers can also be helpful. And it may be necessary to talk to civic action groups, a city, county or state governmental agency, an influential blogger, etc. Your clients will be able to identify those who have an impact on their operations, whether positive or negative. In an Operations Alignment Review they will want to talk to these stakeholders as well.

Pre-session research will help uncover others who have sway over a company's success, particularly critics. Clients sometimes want to ignore critics, yet critics can be useful sources of information. Representation from some of these stakeholders may be needed on Process Alignment Study Teams that may be formed later to study and align internal processes. For more information see Component 6 that follows, on *Teach Process Alignment*.

Finally, prior to the Operations Alignment Review, the leadership team will want to create an opportunity to talk with outside auditors who are familiar with the organization and with similar businesses, because the auditors likely have knowledge of many industries and the outcomes of their alignment efforts.

Outcomes of Aligning Operations using an Operations Alignment Review

Using an Operations Alignment Review to align operations ensures that re-sources, and the necessary efforts to produce them, are allocated in accordance with the vision for the organization. The results of the review will include:

- Highlighting any discrepancies identified by the above investigations.

- Bringing to light any mismatch of hopes, dreams or expectations with daily work life.

- If there is a misalignment, identifying it and suggesting alternatives by forming a Process Study Team to address it.

Here is a suggested agenda for a one-day Operations Alignment Review. A form for the Pre-work Assignment on Role Description also follows.

AGENDA, OPERATIONS ALIGNMENT REVIEW

1. Welcome. Purpose for the Meeting

2. Introductions (name, work unit or organization they are representing)

3. What is our purpose today?

   Our Operations Alignment Review will answer the following questions:

   Are we organized in the optimal manner to align with our vision, and to support our mission, values and positive possibilities?

   Are day-to-day processes working smoothly, and aligned with our vision?

4. Budget to Operations: what functions and initiatives are fully resourced now?

   Which could be better resourced to ensure accomplishment of our vision?

5. Organization Chart: are we structured to align with our vision?

   What are new or modified structure possibilities?

6. New structure, new initiatives, new positions? Engage small groups in creative brainstorming, followed by flipchart presentations to the larger group.

7. Process Alignment Priorities.

8. Action Items. Assign accountabilities.

9. Closing: acknowledgements, and appreciations.

Role Description

This role description is intended to be a general reflection of the functions and duties to be performed. It is not an all-encompassing account of each and every responsibility or task to be carried out by someone in this position. Functions, responsibilities, and duties may be added, deleted, or modified

Position Title:

Who do you report to? _____

Who reports to you? _____, _____

Major Functions:
List the major functions (key areas of responsibility and duties) of the role you play within the Company:

1. _____

2. _____

3. _____

Duties
List the key duties you perform under each function. Provide enough detail for a general understanding of what you do.

Function # 1 _____
Duties you perform:

A.

B.

C.

Function # 2 _____
Duties you perform:

A.

B.

C.

Function # 3 _____
Duties you perform:

A.

B.

C.

Using the definitions below (ARCI), please list the working relationship you have in each of your functions.

Accountable– You own this particular function. This is what you get paid to do or complete.

Responsible – You play an engaged and supporting role for the successful completion of this function (within agreed upon parameters).

Consulted – You are in the loop and must give your approval before actions are taken or decisions are made regarding this function.

Informed – (FYI) you must be advised after actions are taken and decisions are made regarding this function.

Function # 1 _____
Function # 2 _____
Function # 3 _____

Given your weekly work schedule, list the percentage of time you normally spend on each of your functions.

Function # 1 _____   Percentage _____
Function # 2 _____   Percentage _____
Function # 3 _____   Percentage _____

Chartering a LEAD TEAM: Aligning and delivering through shared leadership

To ensure the sustainability of the system's transformation process and the positive, whole system attitudes, beliefs and values that are being embraced in ALIGN Coaching, a small group of employees representing all divisions of the system (levels, departments, units, divisions, work teams) are selected to be an adjunct to the executive and management team. This group should represent a diverse cross-section of skills, experience and seniority from each organizational unit they represent. These selected people are asked to volunteer to come together to form the LEAD TEAM.

The LEAD TEAM is often formed during the ALIGN Phase and implemented during the DELIVER Phase of LEAD. However, as shown in *A Timeline for Whole Field Change* diagram below, it can be initiated at an earlier stage in the LEAD Process, which would allow its members to participate in the design and delivery of the change effort.

The LEAD TEAM structure is steered by a charter known as the *LEAD TEAM ACTION Guide.* This is the WFA operations review structure and process that is used for assigning accountabilities and tasks to these organization members. Their job will then include ensuring the aligning of day-to-day practices with vision. LEAD TEAM ACTION is a competency-based framework used for guiding the actions of leaders and members of systems that are going through significant personal or organizational change.

"Leadership is the capacity to translate vision into reality," as Warren Bennis, a pioneer in leadership studies, once wrote.[61] He believed that the work of leaders in a system is to establish the vision, and set direction, while managers' jobs were to ensure that promised work gets completed. The LEAD TEAM then functions as an adjunct to the leadership and management teams. It might include executives, managers, supervisors, professional staff and frontline workers. It is focused solely on aligning the system with its vision and making recommendations on what to do to move with confidence towards alignment.

The LEAD TEAM consults. Final decisions to support a recommendation from them rests with the organization's leaders and managers.

I have found that the establishment of a LEAD TEAM sets the context for what Bennis referred to as *creative collaboration*: inviting engaged and inspired thinking from every corner of the system. This would result in a partnership committed to both alignment *and* innovation.

Ron Heifitz[62] has written about times when organizations face *adaptive* challenges. Distinguished from what he calls *adoptive* or routine challenges, adaptive challenges are the whole field challenges that you, the coach, are helping your client address, the kinds of challenges that may be calling into question the basic orientation of their system. These might require adjusting to a radically altered environment of new markets, customers, competition and technology; ones that involve defining new roles and relationships, and that tend to demand changing not just behaviors but deeply embedded beliefs and values as well – challenges where new levels of employee responsibility and learning are required.

The risks during such times may seem especially high because change that truly transforms an individual, team, group or organization often demands that people give up things they hold dear, even if not currently working well, such as habits, loyalties, and ways of thinking, in order to gain the benefits of living their shared vision on a daily basis.

Ultimately, the purpose of establishing a LEAD TEAM is to build accountability, capability and leadership commitment across all divisions and levels within a system committed to the goal of achieving breakthrough results.

Restructuring to create a LEAD TEAM involves bringing together

a) The current leadership team (direct reports to the CEO, COO, Administrator, Business Owner or Team Leader), and

b) A selected group of individuals, usually one person from each section of the organization. For the purposes of the LEAD TEAM, this diverse group should be composed of people who have already shown informal leadership and who are committed to the vision.

The LEAD TEAM may also take on accountability for some projects, including research and development. For example, if there is a misaligned process they can charter a Process Study Team. Or they can make recommendations to the executive team regarding changes in rewards for employees. Their mandate is wide-ranging, covering the whole field. Their goal is to bring the envisioned future into the present, initiating and sustaining actions that promote the ability to live now as if the imagined future was already occurring.

A Story about how a LEAD TEAM can transform a system

The CEO of a Midwestern Regional Hospital knew his organization needed to generate a breakthrough to an effective, workable partnership between the Board, administration, the physicians and hospital staff. This breakthrough was one that required an alignment of vision, commitment and core values that had never been achieved before.

Since this organization's leadership team and board had begun participating in The Timeline for Change process (a Whole Field Alignment process), one of the engagements was a whole system meeting of all stakeholders. It was there, at the end of the second day, after all the discussions that had occurred regarding mission, core values and strengths, and vision that the LEAD TEAM came together to articulate their positive possibilities and strategic intention. This could have been a long treatise or a short paragraph, but when the words "Breakthrough to Shared Leadership" were spoken, everyone knew they had identified their path to the future.

So even though the CEO acknowledged that he had no idea what a "Breakthrough to Shared Leadership" meant, he knew that this was the culture they wanted and NEEDED to create there.

What followed was an unusual process: every member of the leadership team asked someone to be his or her coach in learning how to share leadership. The CEO asked a LEAD TEAM member from two levels below his to be his coach, and then demonstrated his commitment by holding regular meetings with this coach to focus on getting help in defining what 'shared leadership' looked like, walked like and talked like for a CEO.

It was an inquiry that both took very seriously, and it lasted until a few years later when the CEO left that healthcare system.

By selecting someone at the manager level instead of sticking to just his own level or that of a member of his executive team, he modeled Shared Leadership. Their declared breakthrough was already in action!

When a West Coast regional mental healthcare system utilized their LEAD TEAM

A regional system in the Pacific Northwest was planning to merge three other mental health services organizations into one. This change was being mandated by the State.

Just a year before, however, they had gone through a merger of two of the largest mental healthcare systems in the area that, according to the CEO and a few members of the Board, "had not gone well."

Now they were being asked to do it again – this time merging five previously independent organizations with their own boards into one.

Not wanting to repeat the mistakes of the past, they chose ALIGN Coaching with the Whole Field Alignment model as their path to the future. A diagram of the process we coaches proposed, named A Timeline for Whole Field Change, looked like this:

A Time Line for Whole Field Change

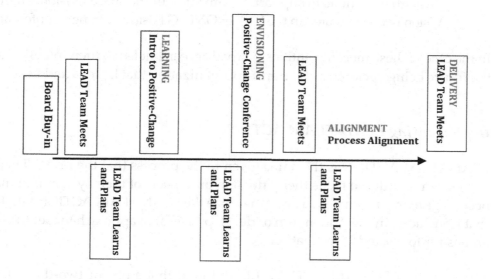

After a presentation to the newly combined Board to gain their support and participation, the CEO convened the LEAD TEAM. Bringing the group together at this time accomplished multiple important goals. These included:

1. Bringing representatives from all the merging organizations together.

2. Creating an internal LEAD TEAM, a guiding coalition of committed leaders focused on moving the system towards the positive possibilities of the future.

3. Introducing the LEAD TEAM members to the latest information on leadership excellence.

4. Engaging the LEAD TEAM in designing the Whole Field Change process, lending their perspectives from every part of the newly merging system.

5. Having advocates (LEAD TEAM members) in the room at each stake-holders' event to help lead and guide the conversation.

6. Ensuring that the LEAD TEAM is up and running and ready to follow through on actions to support alignment with the shared vision. Shared Vision was articulated in the ENVISIONING Positive Change Conference.

In the case of these merging entities, a broad agreement led to their intention for the future being declared as "We are an Organization that Listens and Learns."

Implementing LEAD TEAM ACTION

LEAD TEAM ACTION is the name given to the process that the LEAD TEAM engages in in order to focus their attention on aspects of their system that may need alignment and change. They can utilize the LEAD TEAM ACTION GUIDE that is included in the Addendum or develop their own approach to identifying arenas for focus and investigation.

To initiate LEAD TEAM ACTION, I have found that a one or two-day offsite meeting for prospective LEAD TEAM members is required. This allows the identified potential team to clarify its role, organize itself to take on account-ability for specific focus arenas, and begin to brainstorm first actions.

Here is the agenda for the meeting that was used in the intervention described above. The meeting lasted 1.5 days:

AGENDA FOR TODAY: YOUR INVITATION TO JOIN THE LEAD TEAM

1. Welcome. Engage participants in a conversation about their expectations for the day, and the reasons for their invitation to join the LEAD TEAM.

2. Intention Setting: review the purpose of the LEAD TEAM, and today's goal of initiating reflection on the misalignment between present capa-bilities and the organization's vision of the future.

3. Introduce the Leadership for a Healthy World model (see ALIGN, Component 3), and the 5 Competencies of aligned organizations that are discussed below.

4. LEAD TEAM ACTION: begin aligning on LEAD TEAM accountability for whole field transformation and commitment to co-lead the change process alongside the leadership team and the board.

5. Match each LEAD TEAM member with a focus arena. This works best if members get a chance to select in what arena their passion lies. It also works well to have two people on each focus arena.

6. LEAD TEAM members review their focus arena and begin to brain-storm, identifying aspects of the organization that they believe may need to be better aligned with the vision of the future.

7. Clarify each person's role in ensuring the success of the change process, discuss next steps and formulate focus arena project goals.

8. Set ground rules for future meetings of the LEAD TEAM.

9. Complete the day by declaring the intentions that will pull the LEAD TEAM into action and into the future.

The LEAD TEAM continued to meet throughout the year-long change process, and for some time after, both to learn and to help model the transformation of the system into a learning organization, and also to help plan for the offsite meetings that brought both internal and external stakeholders together.

Their personal invitations to outside stakeholders requesting their attendance led to individuals and groups being represented at the 75 - 80% level, far past previous efforts to get all the stakeholders in the room.

The LEAD TEAM ACTION GUIDE has two sections

Each member of the LEAD TEAM is given a copy of the *LEAD TEAM ACTION GUIDE*, which had two sections:

<u>Section one</u> identifies and defines the five critical competencies of effective individuals, teams and groups that are needed for creating a fully aligned field. Developing these competencies builds a system-wide foundation for increasing whole field capacity, and the LEAD TEAM is asked to engage in building these capacities throughout their system.

<u>Section two</u> of the LEAD TEAM ACTION Guide provides ideas and specific examples of what members of the team could do to move their organization in the direction of becoming more highly functioning, capable and 'leader-full' (having empowered people) – and becoming aligned with their company's vision story. This section contains a listing of suggested actions from which an accountable team might choose, for how to engage others in tasks or conversations that bring the future ideal into the present.

One important reason for applying the LEAD TEAM ACTION structure is that it will focus an all-organization representative group on the entire system (field), rather than on the pieces each employee faces operationally day-to-day. The LEAD TEAM applies the discipline of Whole Field Alignment, and considers STYLE, STRATEGY and STRUCTURE in their deliberations and recommendations. The LEAD TEAM thus has the tools it needs for more comprehensively identifying what's needed to implement and sustain change.

Working with the LEAD TEAM ACTION framework will allow the system to produce results more quickly and efficiently, and to build resilience for dealing with change as a constant.

The first several months of an ALIGN Coaching effort represent your client's greatest opportunity to ignite a new spirit of commitment amongst employees, and engage them in the process of establishing more productive daily routines. LEAD TEAM ACTION, described in the next few pages and in the Addendum, will serve as a useful guide for creatively thinking about and subsequently addressing these vital needs.

SECTION ONE – Building System Competencies

To guide the transformation process, **a structure called the LEAD TEAM** is chartered, composed of the organization's current leadership team plus representatives of all organizational levels and major departments, divisions or units. With ongoing coaching, the LEAD TEAM guides efforts to build organizational competency in key operational areas.

Research has shown that there are five competencies needed by organization leaders, members and stakeholders for creating an aligned, positive, empowered and productive system. These five competencies are: Generative Competence, Affirmative Competence, Collaborative Competence, Catalytic Competence and Whole Field Harmonizing Competence.

Whole Field Alignment: The Five Competencies

Leaders, teams, individuals and organizations that are responsive to changes in their environment, and are able to produce and sustain impressive results, demonstrate competence in five arenas:

1. Generative Competence
2. Affirmative Competence

3. Collaborative Competence
4. Catalytic Competence
5. Whole Field Harmonizing Competence

It is the LEAD TEAM, with your coaching, that takes on accountability for building these competencies throughout the system.

1. Generative Competence: Resilience and Learning

Generative Competence is the ability to learn from experience and apply that knowledge to new situations. Thus, not only is the task accomplished, but creative potential and innovative thinking are expanded as well.

The coach works with the LEAD TEAM to build this capability by helping them create a context in which inquiry and learning flourish. As their coach, by encouraging awareness and flexibility in thinking and action, you help create conditions for responsiveness to new challenges and change.

LEAD TEAM Focus Arenas

Each of the five competencies is linked with two or three arenas for LEAD TEAM focus. Evidencing positive changes in these in organizational life becomes the LEAD TEAM members' agenda.

Generative Competence:
  Awareness
  Learning/Resilience
  Innovating

Affirmative Competence:
  Acknowledgment
  Renewal,
  Empowerment

Collaborative Competence:
  Commitment
  Partnership
  Alignment

Catalytic Competence:
  Creativity
  Strength-based Inquiry
  Shared Vision

Whole Field Harmonizing Competence
  Ecology
  Sustainability
  Inclusiveness (Empathy/
  Community Respect)

2. *Affirmative Competence: Acknowledgement and Renewal*

Affirmative Competence is the ability to focus on what the system and the individuals in it have done or are doing well – their strengths, successes, positive core, positive intentions and potential – with the larger commitment to build self-worth, hope and capability.

Coaching the LEAD TEAM, you would support them in building this capability by encouraging them to celebrate achievements and strengths. By having more empowering views of reality and by setting positive expectations of competence and success, the LEAD TEAM can shape behavior, create hope, and open up new possibilities within the system.

3. *Collaborative Competence: Commitment and Partnering*

Collaborative Competence is the ability to create forums in which all members can explore ideas, challenge assumptions, partner and interact in the pursuit of common goals and new ideas.

The individual, team, leader or organization with this capability designs structures that encourage active debate and the championing of many perspectives and ideas – a continuous, open, active dialogue, that contributes to effectiveness in relationships and positive partnering. Your collaborating with the LEAD TEAM sets up a model from which they can draw to set standards for this throughout the system.

4. *Catalytic Competence: Connecting in the Community*

Catalytic Competence is the ability to stretch beyond "reasonable" limits, familiar patterns or old boundaries, especially in relationships, sparking breakthrough results by inquiring into emerging possibilities.

The individual, team, leader or organization with this capability shares their vision and makes it safe to redefine boundaries, and to experiment with new ideas for achieving results that contribute to healthy systems. As their coach, you encourage them to be catalysts for wide-ranging conversations with stakeholders within the organization, in the community and in the global village, that lead to innovative ways of thinking and organizing.

5. Whole Field Harmonizing Competence: Global Whole Field Alignment

Whole Field Harmonizing Competence is the ability to understand and integrate the whole field to work and live in harmony. Being their coach calls upon both you and your clients to engage the system with respect for themselves, others, the community and the world. This includes holding a view that is inclusive and open to learning from others, recognizing and experiencing the world from another's point of view – an emotional resonance much like "walking in another person's shoes".

Coaching the individual, team, leader or organization to demonstrate this capability is to ensure that they see their connection to the global community and seek to engage ecologically and empathetically at every level of system. They recognize the value of diversity and eliminating boundaries between people and systems, and encouraging inclusion of a wide range of people, their ideas and thoughtful inputs.

SECTION 2 –LEAD TEAM ACTION raises the system's competencies

Part 2 of LEAD TEAM ACTION lists the five competencies and links them to those aspects of organizational life on which a LEAD TEAM might focus. This is then followed by a guiding "Purpose" for those engaged in that focus.

Finally, in the "Overview" that follows, some specific elements of organization life are listed. These are intended to serve as a starting place for inquiry, one that you, as the coach of the LEAD TEAM, can facilitate.

My own experience has shown that this intense focus will be needed to move a system in the direction of becoming more aligned, more highly functioning, capable, 'leader-full,' and empowered. Your client will need such a guiding coalition, i.e., a LEAD TEAM.

Each LEAD TEAM member is encouraged to follow their interests in the selection of a competency on which to focus. In addition to the suggestions given, LEAD TEAM members may customize the list for their arena of focus by adding particulars that might be specific to their own system.

You will coach the LEAD TEAM in clarifying each arena for which they have taken on accountability. Then, using Whole Field Alignment, seek to:

- Understand and assess that arena;

- Brainstorm and research others' (other systems, companies, departments or teams) successes;

- and finally, they would study the various possibilities, test to be sure they are aligned with the system's vision, and make recommendations to your client on what needs to be done.

I suggest that the timeframe for commitment to be active on the LEAD TEAM be one to two years with a rotating schedule for replacement.

At the end of the first year, LEAD TEAM members will have the means to evaluate how far the system has come in becoming what it wants to be, while pointing toward how the system might complete its journey to the future. This raises the level of whole system understanding and accountability for the whole.

THE COACH'S JOB IS TO ENSURE CLIENT SYSTEM READINESS FOR IDENTIFYING MISMATCHED INITIATIVES AND RESOURCES.

Coaching Checklist: Are you helping your clients . . .

☐ Be sure that accomplishing the client's vision story, describing their compelling image of the future, is the outcome against which current reality is compared and measured.

☐ Facilitate a conversation on how the budget currently allocates resources versus how it could be modified to better support vision accomplishment.

☐ Engage the client system in reviewing their organizational chart, identifying whether the current structure is supporting vision accomplishment, and discussing alternatives, if needed.

☐ Be prepared to serve as an expert resource in the discussion regarding alternative structures. Understand the pros and cons of alternative structures such as vertical, horizontal, a loose affiliation of semiautonomous units, a hub and spoke, and front office/back office.

☐ Determine clarity on job accountabilities and responsibilities; facilitate the discussion.

"How do you change the world? One room at a time. Which room? The one you're in."

– Peter Block

ALIGN, COMPONENT 6

TEACH PROCESS ALIGNMENT

Process Alignment: focus on matching daily actions with vision

Some of operations alignment is achieved via participation in Process Alignment (PA) in an environment of shared responsibility for achieving breakthrough strategic results and living into the system's vision. Process Alignment is the committed study of everyday work processes applying a systems lens to uncover sources of misalignment and breakdown.

Misalignments between intentions expressed in the vision and Statements of Possibility, and day-to-day operations don't occur because people lack care about how they work or lack the desire to work toward accomplishing organizational goals. Misalignments occur because most processes and procedures were designed prior to attaining clarity on the client/client system's vision story, and they aren't systemic.

Process Alignment is driven by the involvement of leaders, managers, staff and process stakeholders within a culture committed to inquiry, participation, responsibility, partnership and customer satisfaction. It usually requires training in Process Alignment tools for those who have a stake in the process's success.

The process stakeholders meet and begin to apply PA tools with the intention of aligning the process with their organization's vision. PA tools are first applied in studying the current situation that is deemed misaligned with the vision, gathering data to assess the process (and other impacted or impacting processes within the system) to identify a system of causes that may be contributing factors. Then the system's daily business practices are changed by initiating a systemic intervention to align daily actions with the organization's vision. Experience has shown that, as a result of these meetings, workflows are smoothed out, and relationships are improved within the unit being studied and across the units that were impacted by the process misalignment. Whole Field Alignment and alignment with the vision are achieved.

Groups of stakeholders involved in what I call a *Process Study Team* (PA Study Team), experience the building of the kind of generative, affirmative, collaborative, catalytic and harmonizing competence that allows for maximum flexibility and resilience in adapting to changing environments and evolving business and community expectations. Their engagement in aligning with shared vision, rather than fixing something that is broken, supports creating the positive climate that leads to healthy whole systems. Employees receive the message that their efforts are about possibility not penalty

The intention of reinvention

When your client begins ALIGN Coaching they initiate a personally transforming journey – you are coaching them to distinguish and then follow their dream of a life they believe is worth living. This journey calls for them to first engage in an inquiry identifying personal and organizational strengths and committed intentions, in order to understand what animates them to carry out their mission with dedication, energy, vitality, attention and care, and perhaps even love. The learning that takes place in the early days of your engagement, when ALIGN Coaching follows the LEAD Phases (see Part 3), will result in a shift in the conversation they have been having with others and with themselves about who they are and what it is possible for them to become. Incorporating into the breakthrough the aspiration to reinvent oneself, and articulating it in early coaching sessions, will also lead to a fresh, new way your client can experience themselves and their future.

This period of time is designed to allow clients to reinvent themselves, as they have courageously chosen to confront their own perceived limits, predicaments and limiting point of view. They take on this significant challenge because in today's life and work environments, it does not seem to a lot of them to be enough just to improve. A more fundamental shift in capabilities is needed so clients can achieve their vision of the future. Tracy Goss, Richard Pascale and Anthony Athos in their article, "The Reinvention Rollercoaster: risking the present for a powerful future," say that "Reinvention is not changing what is; it's creating what isn't." The authors also state that for a system to "reinvent itself, it must alter the underlying assumptions on which its decisions and actions are based."[63] In a sense, this inquiry into the traditions and conventions driving the processes is one of the originating purposes for your ALIGN Coaching contract.

Linking convention with invention

After imaging the vision story and creating Statements of Possibility (during the ENVISION Phase of LEAD. See Part 3), you will be coaching your client in identifying those areas where alignment is still needed. You can best think of this time as one where alignment is linking convention with invention.

In the Leadership for a Healthy World model (above, ALIGN, Component 2), the core of system health – self-worth, hope and capability – is extended into the system by celebrating accomplishment, and acknowledging strengths while establishing an environment for innovation. In this way, increasing the sense of self-worth results from honoring the past by celebrating accomplishments, and hope is increased by building on strengths. These contribute to the foundation for establishing an environment for innovation (capability).

In Process Alignment, the importance of valuing what people in the process have already achieved, and what is already working, *before* recommending changes in the process are key to encouraging innovative and whole system thinking.

Imaging a new way of being and then initiating steps that move clients towards a life that aligns with that image can take place during an Operations Alignment Review, LEAD TEAM ACTION meetings, regular team or employee meetings, or during a Timeline for Whole Field Change intervention (see examples in PARTS 2 and 3).

It is at this point that clients would want you to teach them how to apply Process Alignment tools to achieve alignment. Doing so, you may need to take on the additional roles of trainer and facilitator. The purpose of teaching the tools is to enable clients and the client's PA Study Teams to apply WS *IQ* (Whole System Intelligence) in the collection of data, assessment of and change of the work process; they will acquire a whole system view of the misaligned process and its causes, and then apply the tools to develop a system of solutions to achieve alignment.

Discuss with your client: Why Process Alignment?

The following list should be covered with your client prior to initiating Process Alignment:

1. Process Alignment **begins with your vision of the future**, not with the breakdowns of the past.

2. A significant commitment of time is focused on the front end to **understand what is not yet aligned**.

3. Process Alignment **is systems oriented**; you will seek a system of causes/system of solutions, rather than one cause/one solution.

4. It allows for **teamwork**. In fact, it requires it.

5. Process Alignment tools have proven effective in understanding the design of **complex processes**.

6. Processes are redesigned taking into account the **customer's point of view**.

7. The training methodology **transfers to you an understanding** of the overall process.

Steps to creating the environment for Process Alignment

Here is how to get organized for and initiate Process Alignment:

1. Identify processes where misalignment with the vision is occurring. Ask your client what work processes/procedures/activities do not appear to be fully aligned with their vision story, as expressed in their Statements of Possibility?

2. Prioritize the selected processes using criteria such as a) has the greatest impact on the team's ability to serve its customers; b) breakdowns contribute to cross team conflicts that are occurring on a regular basis; c) other criteria determined by the leadership team or LEAD TEAM.

3. Identify the stakeholders in the process and for a *Process Study Team (PA Study Team)*. Units that give inputs and those that are customers should be represented. This PA Study Team is specifically focused on aligning the business process with the business's vision.

4. Train the team in applying Process Alignment Tools and the SIX STEPS OF PROCESS ALIGNMENT, as shown in chart below.

    From my own experience, a minimum one-day training is needed, or two sessions of 3 – 4 hours each, specifically to learn and begin applying Process Alignment Tools.

5. Resource the team with meeting time and access to data. Support team effectiveness with ongoing coaching.

After the training session, you will want to participate in the initial meetings of the Process Study Team as they implement what was covered in the training, to coach the participants through their first steps. This could be followed up with check-in sessions at 1, 3 and 6 months to support your client as they are working on Process Alignment. Install the system of changes that are recommended. Personally intervene with outside vendors and suppliers, or inside units to gain cooperation for change.

First discover what already works

I have often called study teams *PW Study Teams*, adding the word "works" to signal that their efforts are to be positive and focused on the future when the entire process is functioning at a new level. The study team is not focused on fixing, judging or blaming. Instead, team participants are being tasked to first identify what is already working, and then bring a whole system perspective to understanding the entire work process, including what isn't working yet, where misalignments are still causing breakdowns.

By engaging all stakeholders in collaborating, the PW Study Team can seek a system of responses to align the complexities of their work with their ideal state.

Some parts of the training sessions may be in a workshop/group meeting mode with others who are stakeholders in making the process work. Participation in the training can occur either before or after the establishment of a Process Works Study Team.

The Six Steps of Process Alignment

Once the PW Study Team is launched, they will follow the SIX STEPS TO PROCESS ALIGNMENT chart, below.

THE SIX STEPS OF PROCESS ALIGNMENT

1. FORM THE PROCESS WORKS STUDY TEAM	2. CLARIFY THE CURRENT SITUATION & DESIRED FUTURE STATE	3. CONDUCT A WHOLE FIELD CAUSE ANALYSIS	4. GATHER INFORMATION TO VERIFY THE SYSTEM OF CAUSES	5. AGREE UPON A SYSTEM OF SOLUTIONS. GET INTO ACTION	6.CONTINUOUS EVALUATION OF RESULTS
Invite stakeholder representatives into studying the process with you. ASK: What is the history? What is the listening? What are the values and beliefs associated with this process? Notice what conversations are occurring or not occurring. ASK: What commitment are you willing to declare to make this process work?	What's going on? Where? When? Who? What? Highlight what is already working well. Then locate the BREAKDOWN Imagine what will exist when the vision is fully realized. ASK stakeholders: about their requirements. What would the process be like if it worked for you?	Apply the 3 lenses of WHOLE FIELD ALIGNMENT – STYLE, STRATEGY, STRUCTURE in studying the process. Complete a PROCESS FLOW DIAGRAM. ASK: Where and why is this breakdown happening? Identify and understand the systemic sources of the breakdown.	Create a FISH DIAGRAM to visualize causes. Verify the causes with data. Use BAR CHARTS and PARET CHARTS to visualize impact of causes. Decide what is the most likely system of causes.	Prioritize a system of solutions to bring about a critical mass for change. ASK: Are there any constraints? Decide what the Process Alignment Plan of Action will be. Implement.	Analyze progress. Document: Create a detailed description of the new method – who does what, when, where. ASK customers if needs are now met. ASK: What new possibilities now exist? What actions in Style, Strategy & Structure will sustain the change?

The six steps OF PROCESS ALIGNMENT are:

STEP 1 -
FORM A PROCESS WORKS STUDY TEAM

- Invite Stakeholder representatives into studying the process with you.

- Discuss: What is the history? What is the listening? What are the values and beliefs associated with this process?

- Discuss: what conversations are occurring/not occurring yet?

- Ask each stakeholder what commitment they are willing to declare to make this process work.

STEP 2. CLARIFY THE CURRENT SITUATION AND THE DESIRED FUTURE STATE

- Use the three lenses of WHOLE FIELD ALIGNMENT – STYLE, STRATEGY & STRUCTURE (See PART 2) – to get a complete picture of the situation, as well as to create a complete picture of the desired future state.

- Discuss what's going on. Where? When? Who? What? How?

- Determine what is already working well and where. Find out where is the BREAKDOWN (gap).

- Decide what conditions will exist in this process when the vision is fully realized. (What will it look, feel and sound like when the process is aligned with the vision? What are your requirements and the expected outcomes and conditions?)

- Identify what are the Customers'/Stakeholders' requirements. Imagine what would the process be like if it worked.

STEP 3. CONDUCT A WHOLE SYSTEM CAUSE ANALYSIS

- Use the three lenses of WHOLE FIELD ALIGNMENT – STYLE, STRATEGY & STRUCTURE – to get a whole system assessment of the process.

- Complete a Process Flow Diagram, a Process Alignment Tool.

- Identify each point in the process where a breakdown is occurring and ask why this is happening.

- Apply other Process Alignment Tools to identify and understand the systemic sources of the breakdown/misalignment.

STEP 4. FOCUS & GATHER INFORMATION TO VERIFY THE SYSTEM OF CAUSES

- Use the three lenses of WHOLE FIELD ALIGNMENT – STYLE, STRATEGY & STRUCTURE – when gathering verifying data to ensure a whole system perspective.

- Create a FISH DIAGRAM, a Process Alignment Tool, so the team can visualize the multiple causes.

- Verify the causes with data. Some approaches for verifying data include interviews, observations, questionnaires, archive searches and focus groups.

- Use BAR CHARTS and PARETO CHARTS as tools to visualize the impact of causes.

- Decide on what is the <u>most likely</u> system of causes.

STEP 5. AGREE UPON A SYSTEM OF SOLUTIONS AND AN ACTION PLAN FOR IMPLEMENTATION OF PROCESS CHANGES. GET INTO ACTION

- Use the three lenses of WHOLE FIELD ALIGNMENT – STYLE, STRATEGY & STRUCTURE – when planning an intervention.

- Ask what solutions should be considered. What are the priorities?

- Determine how the solutions will be evaluated to determine which has the greatest impact on the process not working.

- Inquire if there are any constraints.

- Finalize the whole system Process Alignment plan of action.

STEP 6. ENGAGE IN CONTINUOUS EVALUATION OF RESULTS

- Analyze progress.

- Assure on-going gains (Is there a description of the new method? Who does what, when, where, why, and how?)

- Document with a detailed description of the new method – who does what, when and where.

- Invite the customer to declare their needs complete.

- Examine and test the new possibilities that now exist.

- What actions in Style, Strategy and Structure will sustain the change?

THE COACH'S JOB IS TO ENSURE YOUR CLIENT APPOINTS AND RESOURCES PROCESS ALIGNMENT STUDY GROUPS.

Coaching Checklist: Are you helping your clients . . .

☐ Support recommendations for the establishment of Process Alignment Study Groups to address process misalignments?

☐ Resource the Study Group members by training them and ensuring they have time and other support that is needed for their meetings?

☐ Understand the importance of personally inviting stakeholders to participate?

☐ Identify the most valued role they can play in supporting whole field alignment via process alignment?

☐ Train members of their system in Process Alignment Tools, and serve as a resource in aligning processes with vision?

☐ To prepare materials as needed for training?

☐ Implement Process Alignment by following up at regular intervals?

SPECIAL INVITATION TO COACHES

The Leading Clinic's **PROCESS ALIGNMENT TOOLS TRAINING** program is available through TLC Publications.

Your purchase of this comprehensive program is a donation to the work of The Leading Clinic, a nonprofit organization dedicated to educating coaches and consultants who work developing strong and committed leaders of nonprofit organizations. See

http://proactionassociates.com/site_LeadingClinic/section_home/index.htm

A discount is offered to our readers.

This program is ready for your use with your own clients, and includes the following handouts:

1. **A complete Facilitator's Guide**
2. **A Participant Workbook**
3. **Participant Exercises, two versions**
4. **Certificate of Completion**

Permission to make copies of participants' handouts is given.

For further information contact

The Leading Clinic, TLC Publications
1180 Central Drive,
Camano Island, WA 98282

or email Sherene Zolno at slzolno@icloud.com

Phone: 206-713-5775.

PART 2

THE COACH'S SECRET: WHOLE SYSTEM INTELLIGENCE (WS IQ)

"Solutions have a shorter shelf life than ever before."

– Darryl Conner[64]

WHOLE SYSTEM INTELLIGENCE: WS IQ

In the world around us what could be more obvious than the fact that change is constant. It's as if we exist in a wildly fast-moving river, and can't casually stow our oars, kick back and just go with the flow. Try it, and the swift current of change would soon overtake, and likely overwhelm you. Getting a handle on change, coaches and their client-leaders face many significant and unique challenges, not the least of which is that so many people are counting on you to help them *initiate and sustain aligned change.*

Many coaches are familiar with the change initiative that doesn't last – kicked off with a fanfare and an event (usually a meeting where some or all stakeholders are in the room), followed by a short period of organizational excitement and focus, then forgotten as the business crises of the day draw away leaders' attention. Given this uneven "hit and miss" track record of implementing change, some may wonder if we coaches lack the knowledge and flexibility needed to be responsive to today's scope and rate of change, especially when the environment is so dynamic.

I believe we do have the capability for whole systems thinking, but the question is, do we *know* enough – do we have broad, yet specific enough knowledge of the system and the context within which it exists, including relationships and connections to other systems – not just to help clients keep up in our changing world, but also to grasp all of what it takes to really make lasting changes that enable our client-systems to leap forward in results?

To achieve sustainable change requires WS IQ – Whole System Intelligence

Systems thinking is usually defined as a method of analysis and decision-making that looks at the interrelationships of the different parts of a system rather than narrowly focusing on the parts themselves. By incorporating a range of perspectives into the analysis, systems thinkers can reach dramatically different views than those who arrive at their perspective from within a limited range of focus. Systems are integrated wholes whose properties cannot be reduced to those of smaller parts. Applying systems thinking also allows the coach and client to take into consideration the interrelationships *between parts* that drive how the system behaves instead of trying to effect change in a part isolated from the others with which it interacts.

Trying to change a single part tends to cause interrelated parts to have unexpected reactions, often negative and destructive.

The ultimate goal of systems thinkers is to contribute to an entities' ability to be resilient and responsive while changing, but systems of any size, from families to global agencies, have a tremendous capacity to withstand change. Often there is the disturbance of the status quo, as described above, as a result of a change effort and then things settle back into their original, more comfortable, but limited and ineffective pattern.

As a coach, you will often be faced with this stand against change, and its concomitant issue, lack of sustainability in a change process, as you seek to support clients in transforming their systems.

Nobel Laureate Herb Simon, an American economist, political scientist and cognitive psychologist, identified intelligence as one of the key pillars of effective leadership and management decision-making. He believed that we needed to gather information on multiple factors in order to make appropriate choices (decisions).[65] Similarly, gathering information from multiple factors forms the basis for the whole system intelligence model presented here.

Understanding of the core components of the system and fostering change and innovation in a system's complex and evolving environment requires whole system intelligence, an important form of human intelligence that I refer to as "WS *IQ*".

WS *IQ* is the ability to assess, understand, change and align a whole system, and to coalesce all of the system's stakeholders, with their diverse dreams, around one co-created and shared Vision Story.

The key capabilities of Whole System Intelligence (WS *IQ*) are:

1.   The ability to focus on the whole that is beyond the sum of parts.
2.   The ability to integrate (and respond to) demands from stakeholders from all parts of the system.
3.   The ability to see the connections between the system one is in, and other systems.
4.   The ability to assess and plan changes that take into consideration the whole system, to achieve a critical mass for change.

WS IQ and Whole System Resilience

According to author Ron Heifetz,[66] there are three levels of change that challenge organizations: Adoptive, Innovative and Adaptive. To be effective in implementing these types of changes, each one requires different levels of WS *IQ*.

Adoptive change refers to change that mostly involves applying something already tested elsewhere into ones' own environment. This might include modifying the work environment to be similar to that of another department's, or implementing technology that has already been successfully used in another enterprise. Impact is limited; and there is minimal risk because the problem and its solution are clear. Implementers find these kinds of changes easy challenges, as they already have some familiarity with the practice needing to change.

Innovative change is the introduction of new practices and approaches to the work of a unit, department or organization. It can have a wider impact than adoptive change, requiring a higher level of planning to effectively implement. Change is easier, although not a slam-dunk. There still is the challenge of the untested nature of what's being implemented.

Adaptive change is highly complex change that challenges the basic orientation of a system that must adjust to a radically altered environment of new markets, customers, competition, and technology. It involves defining new roles and relationships and changing not just behaviors, but beliefs and values as well. New levels of employee responsibility and learning are required that can lead to their understanding the systems problems, identifying the arenas for adaptive work, and generating systemic solutions.

The single most important factor to managing adaptive challenges successfully is the degree to which people demonstrate resilience. Resilience is defined as the capacity to absorb high levels of change while displaying minimal dysfunctional behavior.

Effective coaches, consultants and leaders are capable of resilience. They reframe the thinking of those they guide, enabling them to see change as not only imperative, but achievable (and better yet, an opportunity for adventure!).

WS IQ: Core Distinctions

In dealing with new or growing pressure to change, organizations sometimes must integrate demands from a wide range of stakeholders and make changes in their core processes, strategies and methods of engaging with one another to get work done. A whole-system meeting (sometimes called a "conference" or "summit") is used when high levels of participation and cooperation are required. Usually all stakeholders, or a significant number of their representatives, attend the meeting alongside employees, and together participate in max-mix discussion groups that circumvent normal organizational boundaries. This is referred to as "getting the whole system in the room."

A whole-system meeting may be used to launch a change process, marking the end of old and the beginning of new approaches in organizational functioning. Because it affords opportunities for relationship building across functions and levels in an organization, as well as with customers, vendors and community stakeholder groups, enhanced cooperation is an expected outcome of most of these gatherings.

On the other hand, a whole-system change process such as "A Timeline for Whole Field Change" that was introduced earlier, is the integrated, system-wide, usually long-term, large-scale intervention that is designed to address the adaptive challenge of changing a complex organization, while ensuring that the change is sustained. Coaches need to be prepared to support a leader and teams across the organization going through major change, start to finish, addressing the organization's different components in a coordinated fashion. This is what we call Whole System *IQ*. It is the knowledge and ability to guide whole-system change – systematically.

To accomplish this, a coach would apply the Whole Field Alignment *(WFA)* model.

WFA – *Whole Field Alignment*

Whole Field Alignment (WFA) is a unique, systems thinking methodology allowing coaches and clients to gain WS *IQ* and achieve a comprehensive understanding of the system within which they are operating. It is also the *process* used to investigate and understand how that system works. Using it, leaders can plan and implement changes in multiple aspects of the system *concurrently* to achieve a critical mass for change, and all the while follow their intuitions about what it is in those multiple aspects of the whole field that are most important to focus on now.

By applying understanding of the synergistic interconnectedness amongst components of a system, and thinking through the *lenses* of WFA, coaches gain the key to helping a client-leader move towards achieving their vision of the future. It is *seeing* the system, whether of business, a school, religious organization, agency, or one's life, that facilitates bringing the dreamed of future into the present.

Alignment can be defined as being arranged in connecting or appropriately relative positions; being in positions of agreement, matching or alliance. It is also what occurs when one's behavior, values or experience match another's behavior, values or experience, leading to rapport.

In coaching work with clients, alignment concerns ensuring a match between a system's values and vision and its day-to-day practices.

The WFA model is used to understand how a system (the *field*) works. It has three categories, referred to as "lenses," to study to gain understanding of the system. Worked with concurrently they give a comprehensive view of the client's system. The lenses are: Style, Strategy and Structure.

To be sustained, and, in fact, to flourish over time, the client's field must have a high degree of fit, or internal alignment among these three categories.

WFA gives you, the coach, the opportunity to see the system within which you and your client are working, assess the requirements for adapting the system to its changing environment, and begin engaging in the conversations that inspire and build confidence in self and others. Then you will be armed to take on the pressing task of changing a complex, whole system. Applying whole system thinking using the WFA model, you will become intelligent about whole system assessment and change, and how to coach others to accomplish this.[67]

WHOLE FIELD ALIGNMENT MODEL

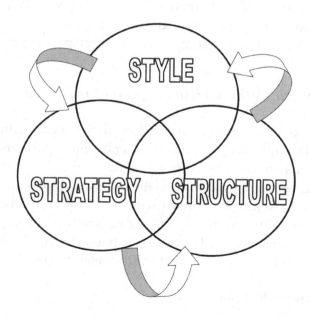

Seeing the System: the view through three lenses

As a systems model, Whole Field Alignment helps us understand the integrated way a system works. It allows us to acquire a *comprehensive view* of the system and expand our thinking about how, in a system, interconnected components sustain the system as it is. Using knowledge from studying the system as a whole, we can then systematically determine how to improve and transform it – and thus dramatically increase the possibility of achieving sustainable change.

This diagram of the field (above), with its three broad components, illustrates the interconnectedness of elements that define a system. These interconnected components are STYLE, STRATEGY and STRUCTURE.

Sustainable change occurs within the context of planned, integrated, systematic change, i.e., aligned changes planned to take place concurrently throughout a system, with changes designed to impact that system's shared values, culture and relationships (its Style); its intentions, approaches to customer engagement and developmental agendas (its Strategies), and its job-person 'fit' and alignment of processes and procedures (its Structure).

Only within the context of a planned WFA change process can you address the relationships within the system and between it and other systems, with *a system of changes* intended to bring resources to every part of your client's field.

A STORY about why Whole Field Alignment is needed

Inspired by some great coaching conversations with her coach, Jim, Rae shifted her business model while also restructuring her business partnership. She had a huge increase in financial results, with sales doubling, and then tripling. Within the new structure, her team was building the skills and capabilities her business needed. She reported to Jim, with great excitement, how incredibly well she was doing, the record-breaking numbers, and her satisfaction at being so successful with off-the-charts sales. Rae had decided she had achieved her breakthrough, and said she wanted to suspend their coaching relationship.

"What else is there to do?" she questioned.

However, after a few months, Jim, in a check-in phone call with her, listened while she expressed being disappointed in her life; she was feeling depressed, had low energy, and wasn't enthusiastic for her business any longer. Plus, in her new structure, she felt that team members were "pushing back" on her, complaining that her leadership style was too controlling and that she didn't treat them with the care, trust and respect they wanted. They also said that she often seemed remote, unresponsive and distant, which alternated with micro-managing the day-to-day work.

Thinking through WFA, Jim responded, "Rae, you've done an amazing job in two aspects required to transform your business: Strategy and Structure. But just like a three-legged stool would collapse if missing one of its legs, I believe that you are missing an important component that needs to be addressed for whole system transformation: STYLE."

As shown in the cross-hatched sections in the "Partial Alignment" diagram below, examining the system by looking through only one or two of the three lenses, which is too often the case in coaching interventions, will fail to provide a comprehensive understanding of what's going on – and likely lead to flawed and incomplete recommendations for change. These are the kinds of change efforts that disappoint us, and sap energy and enthusiasm for the transformational process. They don't take you the whole way; they leave blind spots.

Instead, the change intervention, designed to bring about a client's new field, must be comprehensive, with a high degree of fit, or internal alignment, among all three arenas of the Whole Field Alignment model. This is shown as the center section in the WFA diagram, where all three of the arenas of Style, Strategy and Structure are conjoined.

PARTIAL ALIGNMENT
Occurs when 2 arenas of the system are aligned,
but not all three

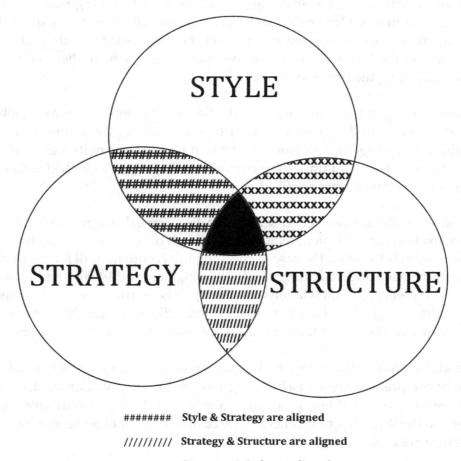

########	**Style & Strategy are aligned**
//////////	**Strategy & Structure are aligned**
xxxxxxxxx	**Structure & Style are aligned**
▬▬▬▬	**Style, Strategy & Structure are aligned**

In Rae's story, Jim helped her recognize her blind spot, which was in the Style frame, and with this new insight into how not addressing the impact of her leadership style limited her, they agreed to re-open their coaching process, and recommit to their ALIGN Coaching relationship.

Components of the "Field"– the WFA lenses

Once committed to having a comprehensive understanding of the whole system, the coach would guide their client to view the system through these three lenses:

1. **STYLE LENS:** This lens includes seeing, interpreting and understanding a system's culture and values, their rituals, stories of the past, shared experiences of success or failure, leadership and management style, and perceived sources of vitality. It is through studying these aspects of a system that we understand a client system's Style.

    Sometimes referred to as "how we do things around here," the Style lens shows us the context within which the client's life/work-life is experienced, their mission and purpose, beliefs that are taken for granted to be true, expectations of one another, and norms for how they will treat each other. In the Style component we see what contributes to, or blocks, trust, effective communication, and willingness to show up and participate.

    Style also includes the identified healthy or unhealthy patterns of interaction between people that either support or fail to support the achievement of purpose and vision. Seeing this, clients can address patterns that are positive or are ones that need to change.

2. **STRATEGY LENS:** Peering through this lens we see the client's intentions, commitments to their future, and purposeful (or not) direction in striving to achieve desired results. Strategy also refers to all the documents that indicate direction: statements of vision, mission, purpose, goals, and objectives.

    The Strategy lens shows us the vision and intention, as well as the direction or steps that can be taken for achieving that vision.

3. **STRUCTURE LENS:** In this aspect of the system we find how aligned work, roles, goals and relationships are with the system's vision, desired breakthrough and intentions. This perspective indicates how life or work-life conditions allow the client and other system members to achieve results.

Structure refers to the way resources are organized into action – what is indicated in its organization charts, policy statements, job descriptions, formal rules and regulations, technology and work procedures that guide people toward their agreed upon mission.

Simple AND Complex

The goal of this whole field analysis would be to use what we view/see (i.e., the data) to understand the system with its interrelating parts. Then the coach, client and the system's stakeholders can use this information to re-design the system, seeking an aligned and sustainable whole field, while also clarifying the changes needed to achieve it.

Using this model for data analysis is both simple and complex at the same time. It is simple in that there are only three components to the field, making it possible to grasp and apply much more readily than other system models, many of which have long lists of components to define and understand. It is, however, complex in that within each component there are multiple aspects, or *sub-components*, which may be relevant at different times.

For example, within STYLE you may be sorting aspects of the system such as

- culture
- leadership and leadership style
- decision-making style
- conversation
- level and type of engagement
- sense of self-worth, and commitment to honor the system's past successes
- sense of hope and a shared vision
- commitment
- shared values
- purpose and mission
- positive and supportive relationships
- teamwork

Within STRATEGY, you might gather data on

- clarity of vision and the vision story
- how aligned internal stakeholders are with strategic commitments
- understanding of core business, and application in establishing priorities and direction
- marketing processes and procedures
- development agendas
- customer relationships and service
- identifying market opportunities
- valuing of employees
- effective use of incentives and appreciation

Within STRUCTURE, you may need to inquire into

- how the current organizational structure supports success
- partnership structure
- structural and process alignment (for example job-person match, organizational levels, barriers to movement of products and services from initiating order to delivery, smoothness of handoffs, misalignments and communication breakdowns across and within departments/units)
- effectiveness of processes and procedures
- shared leadership
- team functioning
- recruitment and opportunities for entry and advancement
- reward system

Different aspects of each component of the field show up as important to address at different times. While a key goal of coaching is to have a comprehensive understanding of what is going on in all three components of the system, getting change processes underway can begin once the centrality and impact of relevant interconnected parts have been identified, assessed and understood.

WFA is a simple to learn and apply model, but it is also one that can provide a comprehensive view of complex systems and a key to what you need to do in your coaching to help your clients align the parts within a whole.

Data gathering: a Field Inquiry leading to whole field understanding

Most coaches will conduct a preliminary data gathering process to help them understand the client system. They typically will use methods such as survey questionnaires, structured and unstructured interviews, document analysis and direct observation. While many of their methods yield good results, they often fail in capturing the whole system's data. The perspectives offered are limited because questions are only asked about one or two of the Whole Field Alignment lenses. The selection of what the inquiry will cover is often dominated by the client's biases, and then further limited by filtering through the coach's own biases.

Here is an example of a questionnaire developed for one client that sought information in all three categories of Whole Field Alignment:

WFA DATA GATHERING QUESTIONNAIRE

Suggested questions for STYLE

1. VALUES

- To what extent are your personal core values aligned with the system's stated values? How do your personal values differ?

- In what ways do you see these values reflected in how you lead?

- In how the leadership team leads?

- In what ways do you see these values reflected in how people here work together, or work with clients (customers, patients, partners, etc.)?

2. COMMUNICATION

- When you and the other leaders are at your very best, how would you characterize your interpersonal communications style?

- What would you recommend that would increase your communication effectiveness and take it to the next level?

- Who else needs to be in on the communication loop?

3. LEADESHIP STYLE

- In what ways is your approach to leading different now than it was before? What factors led to your making these changes?

- Trusting and respecting team members and treating them with dignity are characteristics of great leadership teams. What is a story of a time when you and the other leaders here were at your best in treating one another with trust, dignity and respect?

-   What would take your teamwork to the next level?

4. SELF-WORTH, HOPE AND CAPABILITY

-   Contributing to another's sense of self-worth, hope and capability is a hallmark of great leaders and great organizations. What is a time when your success here resulted from how you supported another's sense of self-worth, hope and capability?

-   What specific opportunities do you see for this organization to increase its positive culture and improve how people here work together to achieve organization goals?

5. CUSTOMER SERVICE

-   What is a story of when you or someone else here went above and beyond in terms of customer service?

-   What would it take for the level of customer service to be significantly increased?

Suggested questions for STRATEGY

1. CORE BUSINESS

-   What is your core business – what you want this company to be known for contributing within its industry, its community and the world?

2. STRATEGIC VISION

-   What would you say is your Strategic Vision Story – i.e., the view you have for the organization's presence in the marketplace of the future?

- How do you want to show up in the marketplace of the future – 3 to 5 years out?

- What will you need to do now to achieve that vision?

3. MARKET

- What are some of the market sectors you want to target for exploration and/or expansion?

- What else can you do for your customers, beyond what you do now? What would delight them? What might going 'above and beyond' include?

Suggested questions for STRUCTURE

1. LEADERSHIP STRUCTURE

- In what ways does your leadership structure support extraordinary growth and contribution?

2. ORGANIZATIONAL STRUCTURE

- In what ways does your organizational structure align accountabilities with your vision?

- In what ways does your organizational structure allow you to take advantage of strategic opportunities?

3. ORGANIZATION CHART

- How would you revise your organization chart to reflect your Purpose, Vision and Values?

- How would you revise your organization chart to allow for even greater flexibility in taking advantage of market opportunities?

4. RECRUITMENT

- What key areas for focused recruitment are needed to strengthen your capacity to meet the challenges of the market? (Probe for skills and leadership needs for next 3 - 5 years.)

- What key areas for focused recruitment are needed to strengthen your capacity to create new markets?

NOTE TO INTERVIEWER: Probe for missing or not well-developed skills, and/or a need to bring on diverse perspectives, such as that from women and minorities.

Increasing WS IQ by applying Whole Field Alignment: A day in the life of the GOT'A Team

Having worked with their coach to develop their vision, the GOT'A Team ascribed to the following:

"We practice consistent and effective cross-team collaboration that supports creative responsiveness to our customers (internal and external) while increasing the respect we hold for them and one another."

To achieve day-to-day alignment with this vision, to add the story to the vision, requires WFA.

Here are some of the ways they went about it.

The GOT'A team had a fairly normal day … for them. Here's what happened:

1. First thing in the morning, the GOT'A's gathered around the water cooler, telling stories and gossiping about anyone who wasn't there that day.

Here is what might happen with a WS IQ – WFA intervention: With insight from the STYLE lens, the coach and client bring this up at the team meeting, inviting the group to think about the impact of gossip on themselves and others.

They also discussed their vision (STRATEGY) and how gossip is not aligned with the dream they have. Then, as a team, they decided to add the "NO GOSSIP RULE" to their team ground rules (STRUCTURE).

2. Their team meeting started at 10 a.m. Their coach was sitting in. On the agenda was "Discuss strategy for next winter's line of Wear-alls." After Angela, a team member, tells them that the new 'in' color is yellow, they all seem to be behind this being their first choice for their line of winter underwear.

Here is what might happen with a WS IQ – WFA intervention: Thinking through the STRATEGY lens, the manager invites representatives from the

Design, Marketing, and Sales departments to join them to discuss color options for the Winter line.

The GOT'A Team decided to make color selection a process they always would do with cross-departmental representation (STYLE). They then agreed to enhance their customer service strategic initiative by inviting key customers to participate as well (STRATEGY).

3. Later in the meeting the manager expresses concern that they are losing too many orders, with lots of important paperwork just disappearing. She charges Fred and Marlene with fixing this problem.

Here is what might happen with a WS *IQ* – WFA intervention: The team, looking through the STRUCTURE lens, think they would benefit from pulling together a Process Alignment Study Team to seek information about how system impacts are leading them to lose orders. Including a wide range of stakeholders, they plan to first learn how to apply Process Alignment Tools to identify what's going on in the system that is contributing to this breakdown. By collaborating, their sense of shared leadership and ownership will be enhanced (STYLE). By including customers in their study of the process their customers will also see they are committed to responsiveness in customer service (STRATEGY).

Whole Field Change: Multiple Entry Timeline

Implementing a sustainable, large-scale change process may require a long-term commitment and include whole field analysis and learning, meetings, seminars, coaching, process alignment training and conversations, and whole-system conferences, both internally and externally focused. Your client may need to bring the entire system plus their Board of Directors together in different group sizes and configurations, to envision their future, and identify the system's strengths and reframe their limitations, and to figure out how to structure themselves to access new levels of productivity so they can positively impact their environment. They will also need to begin generating possibilities – creative ideas about their future – and strategies for aligning with their vision of the future.

The components of a Whole Field Change process, generally speaking, work best if co-created, organized and delivered in a coordinated, systematic process.

To sustain whole field change, the complexity of the system can be dealt with through the use of multiple entry points during the intervention. Although care must be exercised and planning must be deliberate, whole field change is more likely to be accomplished if pressure is exerted on several interrelated facets of an operation concurrently. The parts of the system with which to work are identified by thinking through the WFA lenses.

One of the purposes for using multiple entry points is to build a *critical mass* [68] of energy in support of the change. Just as a chain reaction builds sufficient force to produce a major result, so is a system changed through the development of a strong and building thrust. In this environment, knowledge of the primary aspects of your system, and how to align them is the one foundation to count on for exponentially increasing the change's success rate.[69]

The diagram "A Timeline for Whole Field Change" shows the application of multiple entry process design. This *Timeline* is a one-year guiding pattern I have used in my work with several client systems to design and deliver an ALIGN Coaching change process. The clients for this process included a major healthcare organization, a medical group, a large corporate department, and a public agency.

A Timeline for Whole Field Change

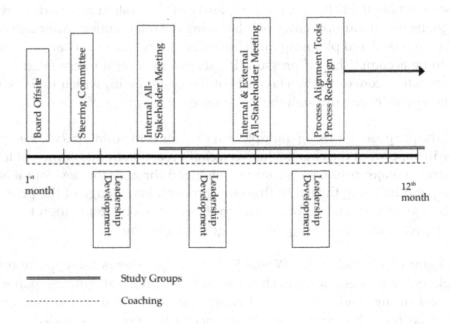

As shown in the diagram, some of the structures for change that could be considered for inclusion in a multiple entry Whole Field Change process are:

STYLE

1) **Board Retreat**: Off-site meeting for members of the Board to align their support for the change process and to invite their participation.

2) **Leadership Development**: This series of programs is attended by an all-volunteer/invited group that includes board members and the steering committee. Besides learning, they also help design the Stakeholders Meetings, where they practice their new leadership skills. This group may be constituted as a LEAD TEAM, a Structure intervention.

3) **Coaching**: Provide key-member ongoing coaching. To establish a culture of coaching, training is provided to the LEAD TEAM and then coaching partnerships are formed. Coaching develops personal leadership competencies, especially in "blind spots," and addresses specific issues within the leadership team.

4) **Study Groups**: Coordinate study groups for ongoing inquiry that deepens participants' understanding of and ability to apply the tools and concepts presented. Study Groups add velocity to the accomplishment of specific objectives,

Study Groups become the vehicles for discussion and deeper inquiry into the concerns and questions raised during the change process. Each person's Study Group becomes the center for practice and application of new ideas, and a resource for building resilience during the change.

STRATEGY

5) **Internal All-Stakeholder Meeting:** Designed as a conference for employees to get the whole internal system in the room to launch the change process. Its goals are to enhance cooperation and build relationships across functions and levels, and to create the first draft of the shared vision story. The client can use this opportunity to give employees a strong sense of the history of the enterprise, its strengths and its accomplishments, while sharing a process to envision the future. The cross-team conversations at this gathering solidify change commitment.

In preparation for this gathering, the coach's job is to assist the client in framing the key questions and issues, preparing to share his or her personal vision.

6) **Internal and External All-Stakeholder Meeting:** This is the *ALIGN Conference* designed to continue to launch the change process, expanding the participation to all system members, including the Board and all other stakeholder groups. The goals are to build relationships across stakeholder groups, create a shared vision story, articulate strategic commitments and begin aligning with the vision. Priorities for future alignment efforts are also identified and Process Alignment is set into motion.

See below for a suggested 2 – 3-day design for the ALIGN Conference.

In preparation for this gathering, the coach's job is to assist the client and the stakeholders who attended the previous meeting in framing the key questions and issues and preparing to communicate their shared vision in a way that invites buy-in.

STRUCTURE

7) **Steering committee**: A group composed of representatives of all organizational levels and key departments is chartered to guide the transformational change process. Sometimes referred to as a guiding coalition or LEAD TEAM, its members are asked to focus on the entire system, rather than on the pieces they face operationally day-to-day. To do this they will be given the leadership tools for understanding, supporting and sustaining change. This would occur in the leadership development program.

8) **Process Alignment, the Process Alignment Tools Training and the formation of Process Works Study Teams** is part of the translation of new vision and intention into concrete mechanisms, such as policies, procedures and work processes that form the organization's infrastructure. How people are participating in the organization, how leaders and teams are communicating, how people are being acknowledged and rewarded, how partnerships are established and supported, and how results were achieved — all are demonstrations of alignment, or misalignment, with a newly stated vision story and strategic intention, and thus are an appropriate subject of a process alignment team's scrutiny.

ALIGN Coaching and Whole Field "LEAD"

WFA is initiated by engaging with your client in a comprehensive series of coaching phases called *LEAD*. LEAD is intended to take system stakeholders on a deep and stimulating journey towards wholeness and transformation. As a result of fully engaging in LEAD, your client and client system can expect to arrive at journey's end with alignment on a shared vision, and continued commitment to deliver on out-of-the-box strategic intentions.

Following LEAD, you will coach and guide the client's journey toward whole field alignment.

LEAD is an acronym whose letters designate a phase that is part of ALIGN Coaching.

The Phases of LEAD are:

> **L = Learn** (focused on self and system understanding)
>
> **E = Envision** (focused on vision and intention setting)
>
> **A = Align** (focused on ensuring that the vision of the future will occur beginning immediately)
>
> **D = Deliver** (focused on implementation of a structure that supports living into shared vision on an ongoing basis)

In coaching, these phases are preceded by the Pre-LEAD CONTRACTING Phase. It is during the Pre-LEAD CONTRACTING Phase that a Field Inquiry and the WFA model are first introduced to the client. At this early stage, however, the client's and the coach's understanding of the whole field is just beginning to form, and therefore is still limited. More is discovered later in the Learn, Envision, Align and Deliver Phases of LEAD.

The four phases of LEAD (plus the comprehensive Pre-LEAD CONTRACTING Phase) are guiding the journey towards an aligned whole field. They do this by integrating the WFA process for assessing the system and coming to understand it fully.

Note: More about the LEAD Phases follows in Part 3: Coaching Your Client Through LEAD.

LEAD is a WFA INQUIRY

How your client applies WFA throughout LEAD

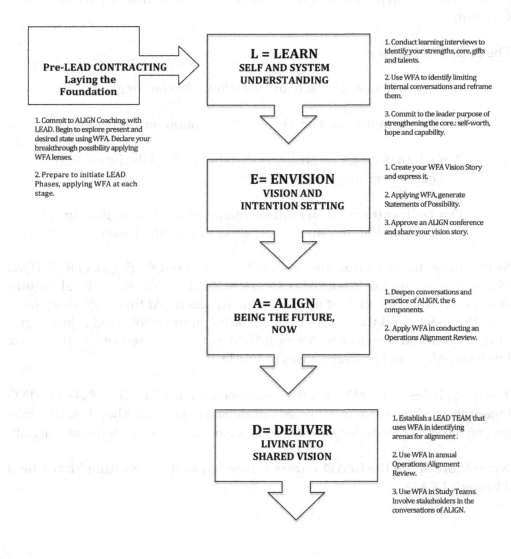

Pre-LEAD CONTRACTING
Laying the
Foundation

1. Commit to ALIGN Coaching, with LEAD. Begin to explore present and desired state using WFA. Declare your breakthrough possibility applying WFA lenses.

2. Prepare to initiate LEAD Phases, applying WFA at each stage.

L = LEARN
SELF AND SYSTEM
UNDERSTANDING

1. Conduct learning interviews to identify your strengths, core, gifts and talents.

2. Use WFA to identify limiting internal conversations and reframe them.

3. Commit to the leader purpose of strengthening the core.: self-worth, hope and capability.

E= ENVISION
VISION AND
INTENTION SETTING

1. Create your WFA Vision Story and express it.

2. Applying WFA, generate Statements of Possibility.

3. Approve an ALIGN conference and share your vision story.

A= ALIGN
BEING THE FUTURE,
NOW

1. Deepen conversations and practice of ALIGN, the 6 components.

2. Apply WFA in conducting an Operations Alignment Review.

D= DELIVER
LIVING INTO
SHARED VISION

1. Establish a LEAD TEAM that uses WFA in identifying arenas for alignment .

2. Use WFA in annual Operations Alignment Review.

3. Use WFA in Study Teams. Involve stakeholders in the conversations of ALIGN.

WS IQ: Roles for your client in applying WFA during LEAD

When first introducing the WFA model and initiating a Field Inquiry during the Pre-LEAD CONTRACTING Phase of LEAD, you, the coach, are bringing a whole system perspective to the engagement, and encouraging the client to do so as well. You will be assisting your client in establishing a broad, general picture of what their whole system is like now and what it could be. A preliminary identification of what would be a breakthrough for the client is also discussed and made comprehensive by how you are applying WFA.

The coach should use WS *IQ* to encourage the client to consider that a system-wide, integrated and sustainable breakthrough can occur when the arenas of style, strategy and structure are included in the assessment, design and implementation of change. This establishes a shared understanding of that with which the client wants help, supports developing an initial set of possibilities for the ALIGN Coaching process, and gives an opening for understanding of what might represent a breakthrough for the client.

The contracted agreement for ALIGN Coaching initiates the engagement that follows. The engagement from the client's perspective is shown in the diagram, "LEAD is a WFA INQUIRY. How your client applies WFA throughout LEAD." The client's breakthrough declaration, formed during the Pre-Lead CONTRACTING Phase, ignites their search to identify system intentions. During the **LEARN Phase,** the client conducts specially designed, positive interviews with a range of system stakeholders, and, applying the WFA lenses, interprets results to identify their own strengths and the system's strengths in the arenas of style, strategy and structure.

Later, in the **ENVISION Phase**, you coach your client in clarifying their vision and vision story, creating a more robust and comprehensive dream by imaging their vision story in terms of style, strategy and structure. As a result, their vision story and breakthrough statement, now sharpened and more systemic and inclusive, can be utilized to form the basis for a focused, whole field set of Statements of Possibility.

A Statement of Possibility is a communication designed to close the gap between the future and the present by speaking of something about the future as if it were occurring in the present.

It is during the **ALIGN Phase** that the conversation about linking the future to the present occurs. When WFA is applied during the ALIGN Phase as a checklist to identify gaps where change or attention is needed, the result will be a system-wide, interlinked understanding of how to make those changes.

In the **DELIVER Phase,** WFA is used by the client as a means for communicating with others about the gap between the present and the desired future. This initiates a conversation for bringing the entire organization into alignment. A structure, called the LEAD TEAM, is introduced into the system, with the client's blessing, to ensure continuous attention is paid to following up on LEAD. The LEAD TEAM will continue to use WFA in studying the whole system in order to make more useful and comprehensive suggestions for change as well as in identifying processes to study to improve the operation's alignment with the vision.

Discovering Opportunities: *Through the 3 Lenses*

The coach and client can continue to apply the Whole Field Alignment Model in identifying opportunities and gaps throughout the coaching engagement. For example, they might realize that some of the following are occurring:

Looking through the lens of Style:

- The client might need a breakthrough statement applicable to the whole system.

- They might see that they want to get complete with relationship and communications breakdowns before moving on.

- They could note how important it will be to develop new, more inclusive channels for communication.

Looking through the Strategy lens:

- They might recognize how they are bringing an operational mentality to strategic issues.

- They might see how those in power (including themselves) may be resisting change, forcing an incomplete implementation.

- They may need to focus their planning for change in order to create a critical mass.

- The whole system may not be engaged in accomplishing the vision.

Peering through the Structure lens:

- The client might not yet understand how vitally important it is to have the right structure.

- The structure might be too complex in a way that impedes creativity and initiative.

- Parts of the system might be inadequately resourced and need to be reconsidered relative to the vision.

The ALIGN Conference, a 3-day Design (2 days total time)
Note: Also referred to as an All-Stakeholders Meeting

While each ALIGN Conference is customized and unique, I have found that some aspects of designing the gathering are important for success.

An effective ALIGN Conference is, at a minimum, a two-day event, with at least two overnights. This allows the time needed for personal reflection, informal dialogue and whole group synthesis. Important work is done by the LEAD TEAM* (Steering Committee or Guiding Coalition), in advance and over each evening, and important data is generated by the larger group as well. The overnight question assignment will shift the conversation towards the positive.

To ensure that you have two nights, the session can begin with a half-day afternoon session, followed by an all-day session, ending with a half-day morning session. It can also be held in a 3 – 5 day timeframe, or over a weekend, especially if the group is large. The process design offered here builds from significant pre-work of the LEAD TEAM (Steering Committee or Guiding Coalition), and requires follow up to ensure that implementation of change initiatives are aligned with the shared vision story that emerges from the meeting.

On Day 2, participants interact with documents prepared in advance by the LEAD TEAM (Steering Committee or Guiding Coalition). These documents are drawn from data gathered during earlier interviews with stakeholders that included positive questions designed to focus on strengths related to:

- The Environment
- Core Values
- Core Competences
- Their Mission

A member of the LEAD TEAM (Steering Committee or Guiding Coalition) presents on each subject prior to handing out a document for the participants to work with.

*LEAD TEAM – the name I give to a guiding coalition, steering committee, or learning group composed of a cross section of people from throughout the organization, including board members and other stakeholders. They have taken on accountability for the success of the change process

Some essentials for ALIGN Conference success:

1. Embed the ALIGN Conference in a Whole Field Change process and have a plan for the next phases of the process to support building a critical mass for change.

2. Communicate a clear and compelling purpose for coming together. This should include a shared sense of the predicament the organization is facing.

3. Get the whole system in the room. Identify the stakeholders that should be included and find the best way to invite them to come.

4. Hold the ALIGN Conference in a healthy physical space.

5. Build into the agenda a means for generating commitment to support the desired conditions and outcomes.

6. Facilitate to encourage deep engagement and generous listening. Model this.

7. Tell stories of when this organization and its people were at their best to identify their strengths.

8. Include time for the sharing of people's dreams and creating a vision story. Let the strategic intention emerge from this vision story.

ALIGN CONFERENCE AGENDA

DAY 1 (Half-day in the afternoon)

GOAL: Shift the participants' internal conversations in the direction of the positive.

OPENING

<u>Leader welcomes</u> and reviews purpose:

> TO COME TOGETHER TO ANSWER THE QUESTION, 'WHAT IS IT THAT WILL FUEL OUR JOURNEY TO THE FUTURE?'
>
> THIS WILL BE OUR STRATEGIC VISION.

<u>Facilitator reviews agenda</u>

GROUP INTRODUCTIONS

1. Introduce yourself to others at your table (or small) group.

2. DISCUSSION QUESTIONS (at table groups or small groups)

    a. PARTNERSHIP

    What is your partnership relationship with <u>name of organization</u>? What is your experience of partnership at its best at <u>name of organization</u>?

    b. EXPECTATIONS FOR TODAY

    What do you expect to give yourself today?
    What do you expect to give to <u>name of organization</u> today?
    What do you expect to give to the community today?
    What do you expect to give to the world today?

3. Debrief with larger group.

ESTABLISH BASIC FOUNDATION OF UNDERSTANDING REGARDING PROCESS, PURPOSE AND DEFINITION OF TERMS

1. Presentation: TIMELINE FOR WHOLE FIELD CHANGE (Facilitator)

2. Presentation: STRATEGIC VISION (What Strategic Vision looks like and accomplishes; how it is different from our usual understanding of strategic planning.) (Facilitator)

3. DISCUSSION QUESTIONS (at table groups or in small groups)

    a. What did you hear?

    b. What questions do you still have?

4. Debrief with larger group.

ENVISIONING TOGETHER

Facilitator says:

Imagine we are in the year (3 – 5 years from now) and have just awakened from a long sleep. As you wake and look around, you see that the people around you, the way things are at work and in the world around you are just as you have always wished and dreamed they might be. What is happening? What do you see, hear, feel, taste, touch and smell? Think about how it is so positive and different now.

Or: Imagine it is the year____ and your organization has just won an award for outstanding socially responsible business of the year. What is the award for? What is said about your organization as the award is presented? What are customers saying? What are employees saying? What did it take to win the award?

Some suggested activities include:

•   Sharing the vision story – small group discussions, then large group debrief.

- Enlivening the visions – small groups discuss specific, tangible examples of their dream.
- Metaphorical presentations of dreams, such as finding or creating (drawing, collage) a symbol for it. This can be part of the overnight assignment.
- Enacting the visions – small group presentations of dramatic dream enactments to the large group.

CLOSE and OVERNIGHT ASSIGNMENT

OVERNIGHT ASSIGNMENT

All participants: Think about and prepare to respond to the positive question.
Note: LEAD TEAM or leadership group with some stakeholder representatives determines a positive question in advance.

Steering Committee: Incorporate input from the day into draft Mission, Core Values and Core Competencies statements that were created earlier during Leadership Development meetings.

DAY 2 (Full-day)

Goal: Shared understanding and view of the future. Creating our shared vision story.

Note: Arrange set up so participants sit with new people, including some they don't know.

OPENING

Leader welcomes participants back.

OVERNIGHT QUESTION

1. DISCUSSION QUESTION (at table groups or in small groups)

    a. WHAT WAS YOUR INTERNAL DIALOGUE ON THE QUESTION?

2. Presentation: REDEFINING COMMITMENT (led by Facilitator)

CREATING OUR SHARED VISION – WORKING WITH DRAFT DOCUMENTS AND ORGANIZATIONAL INQUIRY DATA PREVIOUSLY GATHERED BY THE STEERING COMMITTEE.

1. Presentation: ENVIRONMENT (led by a Steering Committee member)

2. DISCUSSION QUESTION (at table groups or in small groups)

    a. WHAT IS YOUR UNDERSTANDING OF OUR ENVIRONMENT?

3. Debrief

1. Presentation: CORE VALUES (led by a Steering Committee member)

2. DISCUSSION QUESTION (at table groups or in small groups)

    a. WHAT IS YOUR UNDERSTANDING OF OUR CORE VALUES?

3. Debrief

1. Presentation: CORE COMPETENCIES (led by a Steering Committee member))

2. DISCUSSION QUESTION (at table groups or in small groups)

    a. WHAT IS YOUR UNDERSTANDING OF OUR CORE COMPETENCIES?

3. Debrief

1. Presentation: MISSION STATEMENT (led by a Steering Committee member)

2. DISCUSSION QUESTION (at table groups or in small groups)

    a. WHAT IS YOUR UNDERSTANDING OF OUR MISSION?

3. Debrief

CLOSE and OVERNIGHT ASSIGNMENTS

All participants: Think about and prepare to respond to the positive question.

Note: Steering Committee determines positive question in advance

Assignment for the Steering Committee: Based on what you learned in the day's discussion on Environment, Core Values, Core Competencies and Mission, create the Shared Vision Story for <u>name of organization.</u> What is the Shared Vision Story and Strategic Vision that was articulated today?

DAY 3 (Half day)

Goal: Declare Commitment to our Shared Vision Story and our Strategic Vision.

Note: Arrange set up so participants sit with new people again, including some they don't know.

OPENING

Leader welcomes participants back.

OVERNIGHT QUESTION

1. DISCUSSION QUESTION (at table groups or in small groups)

   a. WHAT WAS YOUR INTERNAL DIALOGUE (OR THE ANSWER FOR YOU) ON THE QUESTION?

SHARED VISION STORY AND STRATEGIC VISION Organization's executive tells the Vision Story and the Strategic Vision that was generated by the Steering Committee the night before.

UNDERSTANDING OF AND COMMITMENT TO OUR SHARED VISION STORY AND STRATEGIC VISION

1. DISCUSSION QUESTION (at table groups or in small groups)

   a. WHAT DOES THE SHARED VISION AND STRATEGIC VISION SAY TO YOU?

   b. WHAT IS OUR COMMON UNDERSTANDING OF OUR SHARED VISION STORY AND STRATEGIC VISION? ARE WE COMMITTED TO EXAMINING HOW WE MIGHT LIVE THEM OUT?

   c. POSSIBILITIES: WHERE DO WE NEED TO FOCUS ORGANIZATIONAL ATTENTION AND RESOURCES TO BEGIN ALIGNING WITH OUR SHARED VISION STORY AND STRATEGIC VISION?

2. Brainstorm; then identify Statements of Possibility in the arenas of Style, Strategies and Structure.

3. Debrief with larger group. SHOW AND TELL: Volunteers select one of their group's Statements of Possibility and develop and present a story of how this Possibility is occurring as if it were already happening now. What's going on; what would we see, hear, feel? Volunteers may tell or enact their story in 3 – 4 minutes.

INTERACTIVE DISCUSSION: PRIORITIES (Steering Committee Facilitates)

> **Process Alignment Tools Training and Process Alignment Study Teams –** The policies, procedures and work processes of the organization are the infrastructure where intentions are translated into action. To follow up the ALIGN Conference, employees will be trained in the tools of Process Alignment and selected to participate in Process Study Teams. Each Study Team's role is to evaluate the organization's infrastructure in a specific area and recommend changes to move the organization into alignment with its shared vision story and strategic vision.
>
> Based on the input from the conference, at the next Steering Committee meeting a decision will be made on what areas to focus on during Process Alignment.
>
> List priorities.

CLOSING: BEING THE FUTURE NOW

1. DISCUSSION QUESTION (at table groups or in small groups)

    How will *you* be part of our vision story now?

2. DEBRIEF with larger group

    CLOSE WITH A QUICK ROUND OF DECLARED COMMITMENT. EVERYONE PARTICIPATES.

PART 3

COACHING YOUR CLIENT THROUGH LEAD

"We are a community of possibilities, not a community of problems."

– Peter Block[70]

ALIGN COACHING AND WHOLE FIELD ALIGNMENT THROUGH THE PHASES OF LEAD

At the heart of ALIGN Coaching is the client's desire for significant positive change. Working with clients, we coaches grow to understand that each of them is striving to be a leader – in homes and families, at work, and in communities. They (and we) want their lives to be a positive contribution to the world, a valued legacy. Applying WFA through the LEAD Phases points you and your clients toward that greatness.

The Phases of LEAD (Learn, Envision, Align and Deliver) engage you in a rich and nuanced inquiry that illuminates the system's whole field, its Style, Strategies and Structure. It is during LEAD that coaches, along with our clients, get to build the sacred trust that makes all the challenges of being a coach worthwhile. During these phases we model openness to possibility and the flexibility to change and grow. We arrive into the relationship with faith that our clients can do the same. We bring respect for the responsibilities they carry and we try to match our commitment to them to the commitment they have to themselves and others.

To begin growing the positive core of individuals and systems, coaches will guide clients through the five stages of LEAD, including the four phases of LEAD, plus Pre-LEAD CONTRACTING. This is shown in this diagram, "The LEAD Phases":

The LEAD Phases

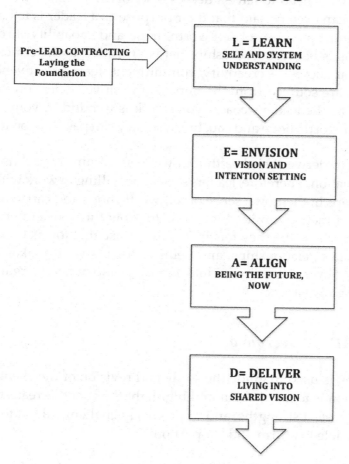

Why LEAD? Yes, it's all about Leadership

In ALIGN Coaching, the words Learn, Envision, Align and Deliver form the acronym LEAD. I created this acronym to help coaches remember what's significant about engaging in ALIGN Coaching: one of your most important coaching goals is to join your clients as they lead – and to help them build their competencies as generative, affirmative, collaborative, catalytic and harmonizing leaders.

As discussed earlier in the Leadership for a Healthy World model in ALIGN, Component 2, leaders need to have a deep, personal sense of self-worth, hope and capability. It can even be said that their purpose as a leader is to have this, and then to extend this sense of self-worth, hope and capability throughout their system. This is because leadership that is affirming is the critical factor for organizational success – creativity, commitment, team effectiveness and customer loyalty are sourced from the impact of positive leaders on their systems. Therefore, as the leader's coach, your work is to build in your clients a deep sense of self-worth, hope and capability, so they can pass that on to others.

People in a system derive their health and wellbeing from this acknowledgement and appreciation. Therefore, leaders should be willing to work with you in examining the gaps in their own sense of self-worth, hope and capability. They do this because of their committed intention to grow this sense in others – in everyone, in fact, whose life they touch. It is this sense that forms the basis for building affirmative relationships, and being valued is what makes possible healthy systems at every level: individual, family, group or team, organization, community and global agency.[71]

Following LEAD: an overview

ALIGN Coaching is used to guide the study and revision of the client's whole field. The intention is to learn about and highlight the client's greatest sources of vitality and greatest strengths, and to positively challenge them to be their best, so they are able to affirm and support others.

This process begins in the **LEARN Phase** of LEAD with a Field Inquiry that engages the client in self and system discovery of strengths.

The challenge to achieve a breakthrough is then used to ignite a vivid sense of what is possible for the client's future. This happens in the **ENVISION Phase** of LEAD when the *vision story*[72] is imagined and detailed. The client's vision story, evoked in a colorful, fully-sensed narrative of what might be occurring in the future, makes the vision clearer and more readily shared with others with a stake in the direction of the client's system. .

Surprisingly, although we often think of vision as about the future, envisioning is actually about the present. It is about making the choice to have your life today come from the future instead of the past. It concerns creating the conditions that would today compel you forward towards your future ideal.

Vision shapes direction, but also influences daily decision-making. It is what underlies our ability to align what we say we believe with everyday practices and procedures. So important are the results of this phase that some believe that people and organizations "would simply self-destruct without a common sense of direction."[73]

So, imagining that the vision story is already realized and happening in the here and now, the client describes what their life is like as they generate Statements of Possibility.

Statements of Possibility are declarations about the future, boldly spoken in the present tense. "I AM" instead of "I WANT TO BE." These statements communicate one's committed stand and connect one's image of the future to action in the present. They are compelling and draw one into a commitment to the future that is being imagined and described.

Taking the client's Statements of Possibility, the ALIGN Coaching process moves forward into the **ALIGN Phase** of LEAD.

Much of the action of transformation happens in this phase as your client seeks to close the gap between their vision story and their present-day reality. During this time, your client will become aware of the capabilities that already exist in the system – what is already known and successfully practiced – and, by amplifying what is working, will move beyond perceived limitations. This often occurs in an ALIGN Conference, an opportunity to get the whole system into the room for a conversation about their shared future.

With increased vitality, commitment, engagement, imagination and energy the client can accomplish their desired breakthrough results. This happens in the **DELIVER Phase** of LEAD. During DELIVER you and your client focus on operations alignment and, working with other system stakeholders, you are both actively engaged in the transformation of the whole field. Establishing a LEAD TEAM during DELIVER can keep the organization on track towards whole field alignment. This new structure of representatives from all parts of the system is often accountable for ensuring that teams get the training they need in PROCESS ALIGNMENT Tools to work together to correct misalignments in processes.

Expected Outcomes from engaging in the LEAD Phases of ALIGN Coaching

In ALIGN Coaching, the expected outcomes of LEAD are:

1) **Pre-LEAD Contract Phase: Laying the Foundation**

   - Commitment to an ALIGN Coaching relationship, and to a breakthrough.

   - The initial Field Inquiry, applying Whole Field Alignment.

   - A preliminary sense of the whole field viewed through the WFA lenses: what is occurring now, and what the client desires it to be.

   - Initiation of LEAD, following the 6 Components of ALIGN (see the chart that follows).

   - The client is coached on:

     o The impact of their conversations.

     o The purpose of leadership (self-worth, hope and capability).

     o The value of vision and the goal of Statements of Possibility.

     o Multiple entry change processes that lead to an ALIGN Conference.

     o Sustaining change via Operations Alignment Reviews, having a LEAD TEAM and engaging in Process Alignment.

2) **LEARN Phase: Self and System Understanding**

- Initiation of Field Inquiries into core strengths and life-giving forces.

- Interviews or other methods are used to engage Stakeholders.

- The conversation, both external and internal, is framed and reframed to one that is more positive than negative, one that challenges limiting beliefs.

3) **ENVISION Phase: Vision and Intention Setting**

- Key themes that appear in the interviews are identified and topics for further inquiry are selected.

- Development of the client's Vision Story. A process for sharing it with the system's stakeholders is developed and initiated.

- An all-stakeholders conference may be designed and held to set a committed intention for alignment with a shared vision.

4) **ALIGN Phase: The Future is Now.**

- Alignment of the whole field with the images of the future is initiated.

- Operations are reviewed and misalignments are identified.

- The leadership team restructures to have the Vision Story of the future guide present-day actions.

5) **DELIVER Phase: Living into Shared Intention.**

- Finding innovative ways to enact the vision of the future in everyday work-life.

- Assembling and launching a cross-functional, cross-level team (the LEAD TEAM) that gets tasked with guiding the whole field delivery on the client's commitments.

- Teams are trained to bring a whole field alignment lens to their alignment efforts using Process Alignment Tools.

The bonus in working through LEAD for you, the coach? There is a deepening of commitment to results getting produced via the coaching relationship. As the coach, you give your client access to an arena of understanding known as their *blind* spot, and the result is that they see new possibilities for action and engagement. Clients see themself *at stake* for a specific breakthrough, as well as for shifting their internal conversation and external actions in the direction of the positive.

Whole field, sustainable change is made possible by your engaging clients in the LEAD Phases, especially when you coach your client to create a powerful vision story that becomes shared throughout their system. Experience has shown that facilitating LEAD is the most powerful tool in a coaches' toolkit, unsurpassed for use in assisting your client to attain a system-wide shared commitment to achieve the desired the future.

The 6 ALIGN Components Form the Structure for LEAD

Pre-LEAD CONTRACT	LEARN	ENVISION	ALIGN	DELIVER
Laying the Foundation	**Self & System Under-standing.**	**Vision & Intention-Setting.**	**The Future is Now.**	**Living Into Shared Vision.**
Build client-coach rapport/relationship.

Commit to ALIGN Coaching, and create preliminary WFA breakthrough declaration.

Apply WFA in understanding current system and desired future state.

Initiate 6 Components of ALIGN Coaching and LEAD Phases with WFA. | Conduct whole field data gathering. Applying WFA: Style, Strategy & Structure.

1. FRAME THE CONVERSATION

Reframe limitations, and shift internal conversation in the direction of the positive.

Use WFA to identify internal conversations.

2. STRENGTHEN THE CORE*

Client interviews stakeholders to identify strengths & positive core, and initiates Leadership for a Healthy World.

AFFIRM | **3. TELL YOUR VISION STORY**

Guide WFA Vision Story process.

4. GENERATE POSSIBILITY

Whole Field Statements of Possibility are developed.

Declare Possibilities using bold, positive language.

Engage in process for shared vision (ALIGN Conference). | Identify arenas for aligning with Statements of Possibility.

Review and deepen understanding of 6 components of ALIGN.

5a. ALIGN OPERATIONS

Hold an OPERATIONS ALIGNMENT Review. | **5b. ESTABLISH A LEAD TEAM**

Select LEAD TEAM members with accountability for continuing to identify arenas for alignment with the Vision Story.

6. TEACH PROCESS ALIGNMENT

Set up Process Alignment Study Teams.

Use WFA in annual Operations Alignment Review. Continue Process Alignment Study Teams.

AMPLIFY what is working well. |

In the table "The 6 ALIGN Components Form the Structure for LEAD," you can see that the LEAD Phases have a process delivery structure that guides the ALIGN Coaching engagement. This delivery structure follows the six components of ALIGN that were covered earlier in Part One.

In the ALIGN Coaching engagement, the first phase of LEAD (LEARN) centers on self and system understanding. There is a focus on Components 1 and 2 of ALIGN: "Frame the Conversation" and "Strengthen the Core".

In the next phase (ENVISION), the ALIGN Coaching engagement centers on Components 3 and 4: "Tell Your Vision Story" and "Generate Possibility".

In the ALIGN Phase of LEAD, during which the process of aligning with the client's Statements of Possibility occurs, there is a focus on Component 5 (5a. in the diagram): "Align Operations". Part of the DELIVER Phase also focuses on Component 5 (5b. in the diagram): "Establish a LEAD TEAM".

Finally the DELIVER Phase concludes with Component 6: "Teach Process Alignment" during which Process Alignment Study Teams are formed and begin their work.

This 6 ALIGN components structure can form the basis for your own design of a Whole Field (multiple-entry) intervention.

A few words about Pre-LEAD CONTRACTING

Having a client engagement fail or end prematurely can be painful. When looking back at my own mistakes in my client work, I could see that the potential for a contract going belly-up was built in at the beginning.

Years ago when I first started teaching in a graduate school program called Coaching and Consulting in Organizational Systems, a visiting (and more experienced) instructor told my class in Action Research that he'd spent three months completing contracting with his most recent client. Until then I hadn't realized that so much was accomplished during contracting, and that a lot *needed* to be accomplished. [74]

I've since learned (I admit, the hard way!) that "if it doesn't happen during contracting (verbal or written), it isn't going to happen" during the engagement.

For example, forming a respectful, collaborative and supportive relationship with the client needs to begin the moment you're introduced, and then nourished throughout Pre-LEAD Contracting and LEAD. Having rapport is not something that just happens. It is something you build toward via your focus on being in alignment with your client.

When filtered through the three WFA lenses of style, strategy and structure, asking "What would be a breakthrough for you?" can lead to increased client system commitment to the full, whole field transformational change process. Having a shared sense of values and clearly stated expectation also needs to be explored during Pre-LEAD Contracting.

The result of Pre-LEAD contracting for the coach and client should be a deeper understanding of the system and how it functions, both present and hoped for, clarity regarding roles and goals, and a growing commitment to the principles that form the foundation of ALIGN Coaching that you are introducing to your client at this stage of the client-coach engagement. While it may be something you are already practicing, it still can be said that, as the coach, you want to be aware of your own biases and conceptual frames, how you are getting inducted into your client's or another group's point of view, and the patterns of communication that are indications of unspoken limitations in your own and your client's world view.

While there are many things that can go awry in a coaching engagement, many of those become moot with complete contracting. So, take your time. Applying Whole Field Alignment during Pre-LEAD CONTRACTING to capture the client's view of the present and desired states will ensure a robust contract. You are much more likely to find yourself on track and vigorously moving forward quite early on in the coaching process, perhaps unlike with previous contracting processes you may have experienced.

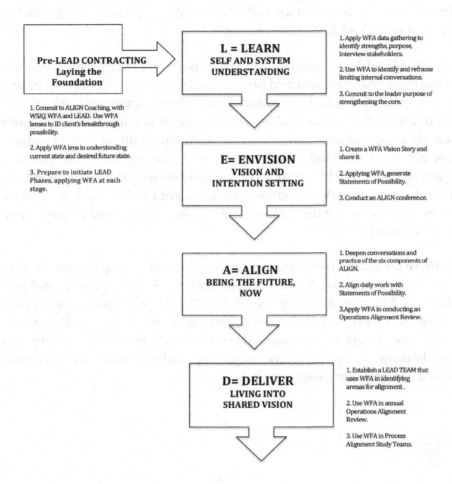

LEAD is a WFA INQUIRY
Applying Whole Field Alignment throughout LEAD

Pre-LEAD CONTRACTING
Laying the Foundation

1. Commit to ALIGN Coaching, with WSIQ, WFA and LEAD. Use WFA lenses to ID client's breakthrough possibility.

2. Apply WFA lens in understanding current state and desired future state.

3. Prepare to initiate LEAD Phases, applying WFA at each stage.

L = LEARN
SELF AND SYSTEM UNDERSTANDING

1. Apply WFA data gathering to identify strengths, purpose, interview stakeholders.

2. Use WFA to identify and reframe limiting internal conversations.

3. Commit to the leader purpose of strengthening the core.

E= ENVISION
VISION AND INTENTION SETTING

1. Create a WFA Vision Story and share it.

2. Applying WFA, generate Statements of Possibility.

3. Conduct an ALIGN conference.

A= ALIGN
BEING THE FUTURE, NOW

1. Deepen conversations and practice of the six components of ALIGN.

2. Align daily work with Statements of Possibility.

3. Apply WFA in conducting an Operations Alignment Review.

D= DELIVER
LIVING INTO SHARED VISION

1. Establish a LEAD TEAM that uses WFA in identifying arenas for alignment.

2. Use WFA in annual Operations Alignment Review.

3. Use WFA in Process Alignment Study Teams.

A Reminder: Each Phase of LEAD should be viewed through the style, strategy and structure lenses

LEAD is a WFA Inquiry. As was covered in the Overview and also referenced in Part 2 in the discussion of the client's role in LEAD, you can ensure your client work is systemic and sustainable by applying WFA in your engagement in LEAD. The "LEAD is a WFA INQUIRY" diagram reminds us how:

In **Pre-LEAD Contracting,** where you are laying the foundation for ALIGN Coaching, engage your client in the following:

1. Getting commitment to ALIGN Coaching, with WSIQ, using the three WFA lenses in an exploration of the present and desired states, and LEAD. Identifying a client's breakthrough using the WFA lenses.

2. Applying WFA lenses to arrive at a clear understanding of the current state and the desired future state.

3. Agreeing on a plan to apply WFA at each stage of ALIGN Coaching.

4. Using WFA as a checklist before moving from one LEAD Phase to another.

In the **LEARN Phase,** engage your client in:

1. Conducting a WFA data gathering to identify client and client system's core strengths and beliefs and values. Interviewing stakeholders using WFA to ensure the questions are whole field.

2. Using WFA to identify client's limiting internal conversations and reframing them.

3. Defining the leader's purpose using a WFA set of lenses.

During the **ENVISION Phase,** engage your client in:

1. Creating a Whole Field Vision Story applying the checklist for a well-formed Vision Story.

2. Applying WFA and well-formed design in creating Statements of Possibility with at least several statements in each lens.

In the **ALIGN Phase,** engage your client in:

1. Deepening conversations and practice of the 6 Components of ALIGN.

2. Applying WFA in conducting an Operations Alignment Review.

In the **DELIVER Phase**, engage your client in:

1. Establishing a LEAD TEAM that uses WFA in identifying arenas for whole system alignment with the vision story.

2. Using WFA in annual Operations Alignment Reviews.

3. Using WFA in Process Alignment Study Teams to understand from a whole field perspective the current situation/system of causes of a misalignment, and develop a system of responses/suggested changes to ensure whole field sustainable change.

The diagram, "LEAD IS A WFA INQUIRY," illustrates how, when coaching a client through LEAD, you can be assured your intervention is whole system.

BEFORE YOU BEGIN 1: A MODEL FOR HOW CHANGE HAPPENS

A story about how the past can drive the present, and put the brakes on change.

In a Midwestern Regional Hospital in Northern Wisconsin, where several years ago the Executive Team initiated a system-wide culture change process to envision a new future, physicians were reluctant to participate. For five years there had been strong resistance from the Hospital's Board of Directors to allowing a physician on the Board. The doctors expressed resentment at being excluded and, as a result, distrusted the Board's and the Administration's intentions in the current change process.

"No matter what we do, they still don't trust us," said a doctor in one of our sessions. Frustrated with his failure to influence his colleagues to support the hospital's change process, he gave us the reason for how others were responding: The Past. "We weren't listened to before," he said, "Why should we expect anything different in the future?"

These physicians fell into an all too familiar trap, namely, to look to the past to figure out what the future is likely to be. When this happens to us, we can get stuck in what we've experienced and learned in the past, with our interpretations of actions and conversations becoming a self-fulfilling loop that prevents change from occurring. In other words, we form beliefs and then our beliefs form us.

And in this way, *our past becomes our future.*

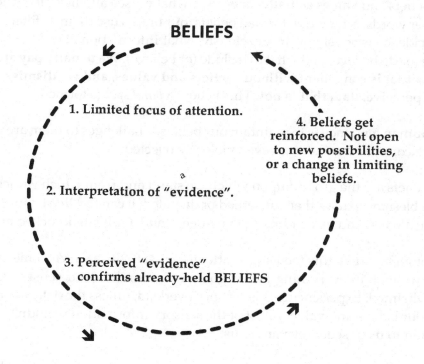

NOT OPEN TO CHANGE

how our beliefs become our reality

BELIEFS

1. Limited focus of attention.

4. Beliefs get reinforced. Not open to new possibilities, or a change in limiting beliefs.

2. Interpretation of "evidence".

3. Perceived "evidence" confirms already-held BELIEFS

Figure A

NOT OPEN TO CHANGE: *How our beliefs become our reality (Figure A)*

Have you ever found yourself in an argument that feels like an endless loop of disagreement between you and another person with a different point of view? So many conversations are like this – a series of back and forth statements of what two people believe to be true … with neither one influencing the other to see it their way. Figure A, "NOT OPEN TO CHANGE" illustrates what happens in this infinite loop of inflexible beliefs.

1. Already-held beliefs and values actually direct our attention; they limit what we focus attention on and thus the information we take in through our senses. This selective focus allows in information that supports our already-held beliefs and values, and filters out what doesn't.

Our beliefs and values actually determine what we see and hear, feel and taste. In other words, after we've formed beliefs, our brains use them as filters to help us decide, consciously or unconsciously, what information about the world to delete (or disbelieve) and what to include (or believe). **We usually pay attention to data that is congruent with our beliefs and values, and we dismiss, or just don't perceive, data that is not.** This is how a *blind spot* is formed.

Our human tendency is to maintain our beliefs. Challenges to them are usually not welcome, and sometimes even violently rejected.

Our beliefs are the ground upon which we stand and from which we act, and it is troublesome to have them unsettled or disputed. It can feel like trying to jump forward when you're standing in knee-deep mud. Or being knocked about.

Although habitual, this focusing of attention is actually a survival mechanism, for if we took in everything that is going on around us, our senses would be overwhelmed. Experiencing this sensory overload, unless the data is consistent with our beliefs and values, most of the sensory information wouldn't even get through to us or seem relevant to us.

2. Beliefs are the truths we hold on to, and values form the rules by which we guide our lives. Beliefs and values are what we accept as the way things are. They govern our thoughts, words and actions.

- Beliefs are concepts that we hold to be true.

- Values are ideas that we hold to be important.

- Beliefs and values govern the way we behave, communicate and interact with others.

Already-held beliefs and values provide the reinforcement that supports or inhibits particular capabilities and actions. Already-held beliefs and values determine our attitudes and opinions. They relate to why a particular path is taken and the deeper motivations that drive people to act or persevere. This is *why* we think as we think and do what we do.

Beliefs filter the data about what is going on, like a sieve. We then interpret and make meaning of the filtered data. You can think of this meaning as like a frame we put around the data. As with a picture frame, our attention is focused on what is inside the frame, and not on all that is outside it.

3. We only perceive the filtered data that, because of how it was interpreted, becomes the *evidence* that serves to confirm already-held beliefs.

We *frame* the data, even though our frames may contain mistakes, plus lots left out of our awareness.

Judgments are made and conclusions drawn without anything or anyone challenging incomplete, outdated or mistaken ways of thinking, leading to interpretations that support existing beliefs and assumptions. Thus is created the mental loop that locks-in the past. The past, our experience and our interpretation of our experience, is determining how we think and what we believe today. In a future that is just a repeat of the past, new relationships, new ways of acting, and new partnering possibilities have difficulty emerging.

4. Having created a closed loop, our beliefs become our reality. We have created a closed-loop beliefs and values system, in which we continually reinforce our own already-held beliefs. We are not open to new possibilities or a belief change.

The story continues

The CEO of this Hospital had led the system in achieving ranking in *US News'* "Top 100 Hospitals in the US". However, he realized that in spite of its success, a breakthrough was still needed – that even though the organization was award-winning, it was operating at a pace he called *HULL SPEED*. Hull Speed is the maximum speed a boat could travel, governed by the shape and size of its hull.

Given the extraordinary changes expected in the healthcare field, he saw that generating a breakthrough, in this case an effective, workable partnership between the Board, administration and the physicians, would require an alignment of vision, commitment and core values that had never been achieved before.

He saw the predicament they were in, that while honoring the past and acknowledging the organization's achievements thus far, to address the new and formidable challenges ahead they now needed what was beyond incremental change. They needed to break with the past by **building an entirely new boat**. To do that they needed to break with the beliefs and values they were currently holding.

He led his employees to understand that partnering could not be accomplished without a major shifting of the relationships that drove the past; they had to engage in a process that would break the cycle that affirmed old beliefs. This ultimately created an opening to restructure the board and leadership team, which, among other things, led to the physicians and other stakeholders being represented on both.

They became aware that *belief is a choice* when they came face to face with their predicament. The predicament they were in led them to become open to doubt that they were on the right path. They had to choose new beliefs about one another and learn to value the contributions that could be made by including others – they had to get on a new path.

The interim OPENING TO CHANGE model (Figure B)

Instead of the process whereby beliefs from the past become the already-held beliefs that drive ones' present-day reality, the interim "OPENING TO CHANGE" model shows the closed loop opening up into a bypass loop.

The Figure B diagram indicates that two functions of belief formulation must be bypassed, and one added to create an opening to change. The two functions that need to be bypassed are: a) the limiting process of consciously focusing attention only on evidence to support the original belief, and b) the limited interpretation that results from seeing only the limited evidence that supports the original belief.

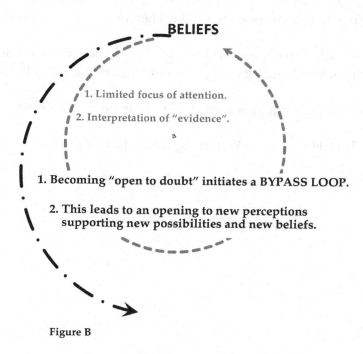

OPENING TO CHANGE

how new beliefs begin to form

BELIEFS

1. Limited focus of attention.

2. Interpretation of "evidence".

a

1. Becoming "open to doubt" initiates a BYPASS LOOP.

2. This leads to an opening to new perceptions supporting new possibilities and new beliefs.

Figure B

The one addition needs to be a process by which an individual becomes open to doubt. By this I mean that something must intervene in the belief formulation process to cast some doubt on what is believed. This is usually brought about by significant change of circumstances leading to an awareness of the blind spot. This is your most important, rewarding and most challenging work as a coach.

So whereas in Figure A a closed loop continuously circles from BELIEFS to Focus of Attention, to Interpretation of Evidence, in "OPENING TO CHANGE", illustrated in Figure B, that circling loop is halted. Instead, a By-pass Loop occurs. This happens when you engage your client in an inquiry and help them see and take a new path that leads from current BELIEFS to being open to new perceptions, perceiving the evidence of some new possibility.

How new beliefs form: becoming OPEN TO CHANGE (Figure C)

I have found that two factors are required to break a self-confirming cycle of a limiting belief: *predicament* and *surprise*. Change begins to happen when predicament leads one to become open to doubt. Then one becomes open to surprise.

This then can lead to an engagement in inquiry into new possibilities, and ultimately into the formulation of new more positive and useful beliefs.

The old, limiting and no longer useful beliefs can be transformed.

The "OPEN TO CHANGE" model in Figure C illustrates this.

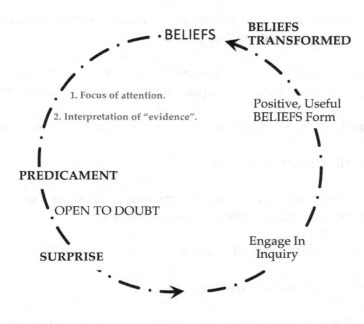

OPEN TO CHANGE

How New BELIEFS Form

Figure C

A predicament is a situation in which a person or group realize they are basically stuck. The predicament forces people to realize that their old values and approaches no longer will help them reach their goals. In fact, the old views often are getting in the way.

For example, at the Regional Hospital referred to above, the predicament showed up as:

- Greater diversity in the community being served that wasn't reflected in leadership and staff diversity in the hospital.

- Reluctance or unwillingness of major Stakeholders to participate in designing a new future for the Hospital in spite of challenges going on in the field of healthcare that needed to be met in partnership or through teamwork.

- Lack of cooperation and coordination across departments that led to costly errors, even patient loss of life.

- Doctors opened their own Same-Day Surgery Center that competed with the Hospital for surgical patients that were financially profitable.

Other organizations I've worked with were experiencing the predicament as:

- A free-fall in financial results.

- Vociferous negative reactions to a management style that in the past used to be working well, but is now ineffective.

- Alarmingly high rates of turnover.

- A vote of no confidence from the Board.

- A significant drop in patient census or loss of major customers.

The predicaments listed above are found in the *external* system. Recognizing these sources of predicament first creates the *opening to doubt*, which ultimately will lead to surprise.

Surprise is *the discovery of new choices.* New choices are options that the client may not have even been aware of before – the options were in the person's blind spot. The blind spot is where the choices are known to others, such as the coach, but the individual is unaware of them.

The new perceptions that occur during surprise lead to new possibilities.

Feeling worthless, hopeless and helpless as the predicament

As discussed in Component two of ALIGN, the Leadership for a Healthy World model is potent in that it highlights the critical importance of having a sense of self-worth, hope and capability, which is the antithesis of what many experience as their predicament: that they feel a sense of worthlessness, hopelessness or helplessness. These feelings are the *internal* predicaments that are what most often lead people to seek coaching.

As the coach, you have access to what your client doesn't know – their blind spot – including, most importantly, how their internal beliefs may be limiting them. You can use the following type of conversation to help reveal how the client's beliefs limit them.

Coach/Client Conversation for Perceiving the Predicament

Regarding a belief you think is limiting your client, ask the following:

PAST

What did this belief cost you in the past?

What did it cost people you've loved in the past?

What have you lost because of this belief?

PRESENT

What is this belief costing you in the present?

What is it costing people you care about in the present?

What are you losing now because of this belief?

FUTURE

What will this belief cost you one, three, five, and 10 years from now?

What will it cost people you care about one, three, five, and 10 years from now?

What might you lose in the future if you hold on to this belief?

A story about listening for, and recognizing the predicament

Kyle came into Jim's office complaining about the people he worked with. According to Kyle, the leaders "didn't know what they were doing." His co-workers were "a bunch of losers," he said, as he continued describing how their incompetence impacted him and thwarted his ability to be successful.

In the middle of this angry outburst, when talking about how he was being limited by others, he said, "Because of them, I am a loser, too."

The coach recognized this as a limiting belief statement: the client's predicament was that he was having a negative internal conversation about himself ("I'm a loser,"), and his feeling of worthlessness was being projected onto others. This kept him from having a positive relationship with his boss and coworkers. His negative projection hid the reality of others.

This also indicated to the coach that the surprise of new possibilities would be that in shifting Kyle's inner dialogue about himself and others towards the positive, he would experience an increased sense of self-worth, hope and capability – and an improvement in his work and relationships.

What "prize" is the client getting from holding onto limiting beliefs?

If delving into more detail about the client's beliefs doesn't create an opening to pursue new knowledge, consider exploring what is called *secondary gains*. Secondary gains are the "benefits" or prizes that people get from NOT overcoming their limitations. They are the filters that keep someone from embracing new possibilities.

This occurs where an apparently negative or problematic behavior or belief actually provides *a positive* or *beneficial end result* in some way. For example, a client may say they want to share responsibilities with stakeholders, but that would mean they would have to learn new skills – it would be easier not to "rock the boat". Or they fear looking uninformed, weak or stupid.

Filtering is not a passive activity. We actively scan for evidence to confirm our existing worldviews, thereby creating the self-fulfilling prophecies that form the illusion of an objective experience of reality.

Use some of the following questions to elicit secondary gains:

Conversation for Uncovering Secondary Gains*

When coaching a client with a belief that you think is keeping them from changing to a healthier whole system, ask the following:

- How does having this belief (the present state) benefit you?

- What have you used this belief (the present state) to get?

- What have you used this belief (the present state) to avoid?

- What would you have to face if you didn't have this belief (present state)?

- What have you used this belief (the present state) to justify?

- What have you used this belief (the present state) to be/do/have?

- What have you used this belief (the present state) to not be/do/have?

*I want to thank my mentor, Robert Dilts, of the Dynamic Learning Center, for my understanding of Secondary Gain.

John Seely Brown, former chief scientist at Xerox PARC, once said, "Instead of pouring knowledge into people's heads, you need to help them grind a new set of eyeglasses so they can see the world in a new way. That involves challenging the implicit assumptions that have shaped the way people looked at things."[75]

Thus, awareness of their predicament and the learning about positive alternatives, while necessary, may not be sufficient to assure a change in beliefs and values – especially when they are often deeply held, even unconscious, and may be long-practiced habits of thinking and feeling related to a sense of identity and power. You may point out alternatives to your client, but they still may not feel there is a *choice*. Alternatives are external to a person; choices are internal. To move from an offered alternative to a perceived choice, the new possibilities need to become integrated into the client's internal sense of the world.

As shown in the "OPEN TO CHANGE" model in Figure C, SURPISE leads to being open to engage in an inquiry process. This inquiry process is conducted via LEAD.

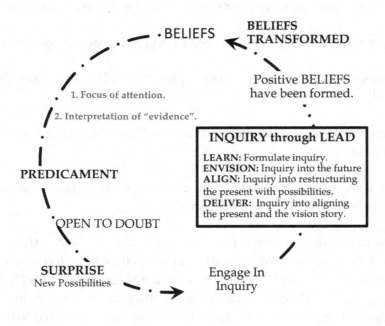

OPEN TO BELIEF CHANGE with LEAD

How old BELIEFS are Transformed.

• BELIEFS

BELIEFS TRANSFORMED

1. Focus of attention.

2. Interpretation of "evidence".

Positive BELIEFS have been formed.

PREDICAMENT

INQUIRY through LEAD

LEARN: Formulate inquiry.
ENVISION: Inquiry into the future
ALIGN: Inquiry into restructuring
the present with possibilities.
DELIVER: Inquiry into aligning
the present and the vision story.

OPEN TO DOUBT

SURPRISE
New Possibilities

Engage In
Inquiry

Figure D

As shown in Figure D, "OPEN TO BELIEF CHANGE with LEAD", new possibilities are pursued via an ALIGN Coaching engagement in LEAD. Through the

LEAD Phases of LEARN (formulating and engaging in an inquiry), ENVISION (inquiring into the future and engaging the entire system in creating a shared dream of the future), ALIGN (applying the style, strategy and structure lenses to restructuring the present to align with the vision of the future) and DELIVER (inquiring into how to develop a transformed whole field to bring new possibilities into the present), a new set of beliefs and values, ones that are more positive, healthy, and useful, can be generated. Thus, old beliefs are transformed.

Possibilities are created by reframing the predicament

As coaches, we assist clients in breaking with the past by first helping them articulate their predicaments, sometimes thought of as the 'punishments' they will experience from not changing. However, continuously focusing on *what isn't working* is less likely to lead to whole-hearted commitment to transformation than focusing on *what is working*. This can be characterized as the difference between working on *fixing the problem* versus engaging in *creating what we want*.

Examples of positive predicaments seen in ALIGN Coaching engagements:

- Employees are demonstrating significant skills and interests in new challenges.

- New markets have opened that are exciting to the client, and that they want to pursue.

- Team members are proud of their accomplishments and want to strive for a 'Best Places to Work' designation.

This is not to say that only the positive will generate the creative alignment your client seeks. Positivity alone, without negativity, can be too much of a good thing, according to research presented by Barbara Fredrickson, Ph.D., presented at the 2005 American Psychological Association's annual convention. She found that the negative acts as an anchor to reality, while the positive led to flourishing and becoming the best one can be.

Arriving at beliefs and values that support transformational change is therefore not about eliminating the negative; it is about how the positive and negative are balanced, or imbalanced. Fredrickson's research showed that there needs to be an *imbalanced* ratio of positive to negative, closer to a minimum of three positives to one negative (3:1). Not ignoring or denying problems or negative predicaments, but rather ensuring an *imbalance* of positive to negative is what leads to the greatest opening for change in the system. [76]

Reframing the predicament – shifting from negative or limiting beliefs to an *emphasis* on positive ones – can lead to this desired imbalance.

Our brains make sense of the world by *framing*, putting the input we get through our senses into different contexts to create meaning. Certain aspects of our experience are framed, i.e., brought into the foreground; others are left in the background. *Reframing* is a strategy for changing the frame in which a person perceives something in order to change the meaning. When the meaning changes, the person's responses and behaviors also change.

Reframing is a process for widening the context or changing the meaning of a situation, in order to sense new connections between seemingly diverse and unconnected elements. From these connections, you are able to guide your clients in seeking possible new meanings and formulating new beliefs that have the potential of leading to new behavioral choices.

The purpose of reframing is to break the hold of beliefs that are no longer useful, and to move towards embracing new, more positive and more helpful beliefs. In a team, organization, community, and in the world, this means reframing limiting beliefs to those positive ones that increase the system's sense of self-worth, hope and capability.

Here are some examples of reframes that emphasize the positive for predicaments our clients faced:

1. Diversity in our staffing and management will allow us to understand and best serve our diverse community.

2. While there are significant challenges to remaining at the top of our field, we have the skills, creative capabilities and the will to address them.

3. The board isn't giving you that critique to upset you. Rather, they believe that useful feedback for someone at your level is supposed to be challenging.

4. Turnover, while costly, represents an opportunity to bring in people who are excited about our new product line.

In the "OPEN FOR CHANGE" model, once the client is made aware of new possibilities (at the point of SURPRISE), opportunities for reframing occur throughout the subsequent LEAD Phases.

BEFORE YOU BEGIN 2: COACHING THE COACH THROUGH CHANGE

In coaching coaches I have learned that there are really good reasons to be open to being coached yourself: before you can coach others in changing limiting beliefs, having clarified your own set of beliefs is essential so that you and a potential client can get clear on what you are bringing to the table. Also, you will have the confidence that, having done it yourself, you can (and should) be uncompromising in asking your client to go through the belief-examination process. You will know from your own experience that it will be critically important for them, and a fundamental factor in making a difference in their lives. Since you will know its challenges and rewards, it will be "Me first, then you."

Otherwise, no real understanding occurs of what it really takes to effect change – and then, when a client resists change (and who doesn't?), your response won't stand on firm theoretical ground. You may come across as having little experience or as being naïve, or a tyrant. You just won't have the credibility needed to be trusted to be with your client as they confront their deepest fears.

Having a theory of how change happens, such as was just presented in the discussion on the "Open to Change" model, means you and your clients can be clear on who you are, and what beliefs and values you are bringing into the coaching relationship. You achieve this by examining your own limiting beliefs and how they may have been formed – and for this you need a coach or mentor yourself who can access your blind spot. This is how you come to understand what creates the conditions for really deep, sustainable and transformational change.

The practice of ALIGN Coaching asks you to commit to creating healthy whole systems, beginning with your own.

The following sections delineate when goes on in each of the LEAD Phases.

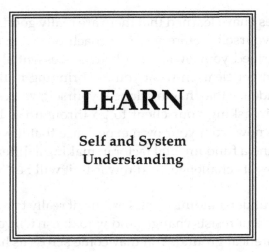

LEARN

Self and System
Understanding

LEARN PHASE

In the LEARN Phase, you will work with your client to identify their strengths and the sources of their vitality. They conduct a series of interviews with their stakeholders called the *Whole Field Inquiry*, and use the data gathered to inform their understanding of their own strengths.

The learning of this phase comes via positive storytelling, rather than from asking "why" or "why not" questions. Interview questions often begin with "Tell me a story about …" followed by asking for the interviewees best, most positive experience in a particular area of inquiry. One example is: "When we (or you) are at our (or your) very best, what do you see as the unique factor that defines us (or you)? Without this, we (you) couldn't even be in business doing what we (you) do."

In the box below is a sample Whole Field Inquiry on leadership.

At the end of the interview, the client invites stakeholders to share their wishes for the client system's positive future, contributing creative ideas to the client's own inquiry about what their future could be.

It is in the LEARN Phase, as a result of the positive, story-focused interviews and your coaching, that the client can begin to expand from their own personal inquiry to deeply engage the whole system in the change process.

Expect that both those interviewed (system stakeholders) and your client will be personally transformed by the level of conversation and relationship engendered by the stories being shared by others.

Generally speaking, the Whole Field Inquiry helps your client gain insight into:

1. The most successful time in the life or career of those interviewed.
2. The strengths and values of those interviewed.
3. The client's most significant strengths and values, and the key to their being able to be at their best.
4. What would take the client's life or work to the next level.

To be able to conduct the LEARN Phase interviews well, the client first needs to understand the power of *positive discourse*. They need to have begun to shift the emphasis of their internal and external conversations towards the positive, as was discussed earlier.

Also included in the LEARN Phase is the deepening of commitment to results being produced via the coaching relationship. As the coach, you give your client access to an arena of understanding that is their *blind* spot *(predicament)*, and, as a result of getting this new perspective, your client begins to see new possibilities for action and engagement.

The client becomes "at stake" (accountable and responsible) for a specific breakthrough, as well as for shifting their internal conversation and external actions in the direction of the positive.

Sample Questions for a Whole Field Inquiry:

Questions asked about the interviewee, focused on their experience . . .

1) Please tell a personal story of a time when you were in a leadership role where you were incredibly successful. This would be a story about when you were at your inspired best, doing what you always dreamed you could to make a difference in the world.

   What was it about you that made that exceptional experience possible?

2) What is a story of how you brought your authentic self to heal or resolve a challenging situation – when who and how you were being, and how you used your sense of yourself, allowed you to experience this vast improvement?

3) What is your story about a time when you did your best work; when you were all-in, and what you did was amazing, unique and heartfelt?

Questions that are asked of the interviewee but are focused on your client . . .

1) What would you consider to be the one factor that gives a spark of vitality to my work — without this, it wouldn't even be possible for me to do what I do?

2) What would you hope and want for me that would take me to the next level, making my life and work even more vital and alive?

3) What positive values do I demonstrate in our interactions and that you see me demonstrating in my interactions with others?

4) What special thing do I contribute that makes the world a better place?

5) How can I contribute more to making your world a better place?

SUMMARY, Whole Field Alignment in the LEARN Phase

As the coach, in each step of the LEARN Phase, you will want to work with your client to:

Style:

- Increase deeply connected, positive conversation.
- Have them tell their highpoint story about what gives life and vitality to them.
- Have them ask for stakeholders' stories that highlight a high spot/ best moment/most successful time.
- Ensure they fully engage the whole system.
- Identify their core strengths and capabilities, talents and skills.
- Increase their sense of self-worth, hope and capability.
- Identify the client's predicament and surprise.

Strategy:

- Become committed to being open to coaching and to choosing the positive as the focus of their inquiry.
- Identify and commit to a breakthrough.
- Clarify the contribution they're making/want to be making.
- Identify system stakeholders and engage them in exploring the possibilities of the future.

Structure:

- Commit to having a coaching relationship with you.
- Implement new structures and processes to engage their whole system.
- Build system stakeholders' support for transformation.
- Set up a structure for Whole Field Inquiry.
- Create a container for a system-wide conversation about what is most highly valued and what is its core identity.

ENVISION

**Vision &
Intention Setting**

ENVISION PHASE

Although we often think of a vision as about the future, it is actually more related to the present. It is about making the choice to have your everyday life sourced from the future instead of the past. The ENVISION Phase concerns imagining the future ideal and articulating it in a vision story. With that as a guide, the client system can begin creating the conditions here and now that would compel it forward from today towards that future ideal. We call this *how your image of the future creates the present.*

Vision shapes direction, but also influences daily decision-making. It is what underlies our ability to align our espoused values (what we *say* we believe) with everyday practices and procedures (what we actually *do*)[77]. So important are the results of this phase that some theorists believe that people and organizations "would self-destruct without a common sense of direction."[78]

Arriving at a clear vision is the foundation of transformation. In the LEAD Process, your client's vision births their possibilities.

Using imagination in the Envision Phase

In the Envision Phase, the client and coach establish the "background" for the client's creative vision of the future, their vision story. This is accomplished via an in-depth review of the learning that came out of the stakeholders' interviews held in the LEARN Phase: best quotes, most highly valued insights from stakeholders' stories, identification of client strengths, and the hopes their stakeholders have for increasing their own and their system's life and vitality.

Then, in LEAD, other applications of imagination that you could introduce and facilitate at this point can include processes such as

- "Breakthrough Declaration" (Client articulates a bold statement of intended accomplishment as if it was happening now.);

- "Best Self Portrait" (Client clarifies who they are when they are at their very best.);

- "Imagined Future" (A guided process during which the client imagines their future/their dream of the future),

- Sensory Imagination (Exploring the context of ones' vision through all the senses and the three Whole Field Alignment lenses.

Any or all of these approaches will expand your client's vision story by imagining it in all the senses and through style, strategy and structure, and will help you to guide your client to imagine a *well-formed vision story.*

A vision story is story-telling that creates a more complete and thus more vibrant picture of the future. A vision story is more powerful than just a vision statement.

A well-formed vision story would reference the client's past achievements, strengths, wishes, and themes/topics of inquiry, what moves them, their highest values, and what elicits their passion and creativity.

A vision story is considered well-formed if it is:

- Declared in the present tense.
- Positive.
- Bold.
- Experienced in all five senses.
- Sorted through the three lenses of Whole Field Alignment.
- Something passionately desired.
- A fit with their values, hopes and dreams.
- Inclusive of hopes for the future, both the client's and their stakeholders'.

Best structure and conditions for Statements of Possibilities

Equally important in the ENVISION Phase is the development of *Statements of Possibility*. These are declarations that when made by the client, communicate their unqualified commitment to achieve their vision. This is often called their *committed stand*. It is intended to connect their positive image of the future to some positive action that would be carried out in the present.

Each Statement of Possibility describes the ideal future as if it were occurring right now. It operates like a bridge, linking what is with what could be. A Statement of Possibility points toward what an individual could *and will* do today that would be a first (or further) step towards achieving the envisioned future state. And then it stimulates further action.

Possibility Statements describe in detail how the future, *and the present,* will be. They set the context for action today to bring about positive new behaviors and conversations. As one of my clients once said, "Possibility Statements are a game changer."

Examples of Whole Field Statements of Possibility

To be a comprehensive, systemic guide that influences everyday work and life, there needs to be several Statements of Possibility, some in each of the Whole Field Alignment frames of style, strategy and structure. I recommend a minimum of three statements each in one of the style, strategy and structure arenas. In addition, the conditions for a well-formed Statement of Possibility are:

A Statement of Possibility needs to be:

☐ Stated in the present tense.

☐ Stated in positive, bold terms, using all senses—what they will see, feel, hear, taste and imagine/think when the desired future is achieved.

☐ A stretch into the future; the client will want to seek to live it every day.

☐ A means for shifting attention onto the positive and interrupting the status quo.

☐ Grounded in the client's strengths and the knowledge that they have already been or done this. The ideal is a real possibility because the client has evidence that it has already been done, somewhere at some time, either by them or someone else.

☐ Something the client really wants. It fits their values, hopes and dreams. It is what is *theirs to do*.

☐ Fits into at least one lens of the Whole Field Alignment model (Style, Strategy, Structure). There should be some Statements of Possibility for each component of the Whole Field Alignment model to ensure the client's whole field is involved.

☐ Inclusive of others. Aligned with the client's wishes and those of their stakeholders.

☐ About how the client can be the person they have always dreamt of being.

☐ Pointing to what is "theirs to do" rather than just what they are good at.

Here is how the future is being imagined when viewed through the Whole Field Alignment lenses, by actual coaches, clients, an intentional community and a religious community:

Some recent Statements of Possibility generated by other coaches:

STYLE

1) I am committed to going beyond business as usual to provide value to my clients.

2) I take responsibility for having an accurate self-image, owning my impact and point of view.

3) I am seriously committed to bringing my "A" game to my coaching with each and every client. I know we are going to do great work together.

STRATEGY

1) I am 100% committed to my client's commitments, and to expanding their map of the world.

2) I reframe limitations towards the positive to increase the client's potential to achieve their dreams.

3) My value in the market centers around my experience, knowledge, ability to bring forward breakthough results, and my focus on client strengths and passions.

STRUCTURE

1) I construct a clear contract with my client and their whole system. I help the client clarify roles and goals, build skills, ensure job fit, and increase teamwork.

2) I follow the LEAD Process when coaching.

3) My team is disciplined and committed to helping clients achieve exceptional results while becoming leaders with a sense of self-worth, hope and capability.

Statements of Possibility generated by recent clients:

STYLE

1) I collaborate with people I trust to create a healing environment.

2) I open others to new ideas, and to wonder, and encouage them to innovate in artistic ways to achieve their dreams.

3) I have an unstoppable work ethic, and a yearning to learn, apply, adapt, grow my people and business and stay on top of the latest developments.

STRATEGY

1) I work one-on-one with people using my original processes.

2) I submit articles to leading journals which are always accepted and published by these professional publications.

3) I am a master communicator, skillful in influencing and reading people. I listen generously with sincere curiosity.

STRUCTURE

1) I hire only those people who share my same desire to grow personally and professionally.

2) Others and I form a Cooperative with shared space where we inspire one another to produce exceptional art.

3) I have the right business structure that allows us to scale up and grow while consistently delivering the highest quality service to our customers.

Statements of Possibility from an intentional community I worked with[79] :

STYLE

1) We are fully responsible for our own lives.

2) We feel free to live where we want and to come and go as we please.

STRATEGY

1) We are secure knowing how important our well-being is to others.

2) We live our lives as part of a whole.

STRUCTURE

1) We maintain a beautiful, clean and healthy environment within which to live.

2) Those who love doing it maintain our environment.

Statements of Possibility from a religious community:

And, after a six-month renewal process, **a religious community** declared the following Possibility Statements:

Honoring Diversity: Many people, many voices.

- We are a welcoming community, responsive to diverse needs.
- We listen to one another, and feel honored to be connected to those who differ from us. We know we can learn from one another.
- We recognize the miracle of our being together on this beautiful island, and celebrate the opportunity to have a positive impact on our community.

Our History and Culture

- We are strongly connected to our spiritual heritage while being open to creating new traditions to meet our present needs.
- Our programs and conversations on our history and culture are engaging, intellectually stimulating, richly rewarding and often focused on contemporary issues. They feature guest speakers, and local talent, including artists, writers, philosophers and educators from our own island community.
- Our programs are also an entertaining, joyful and fun way to connect us to one another.
- Our programs occur in an environment of integrity, trust, respect and openness to learning from one another.

Leadership and Administration

- Our leaders are strong, thoughtful, competent, experienced, creative and positive.
- Committed, passionate and engaged volunteers step in to serve on committees, bringing vitality and informal leadership to get things done.
- Our active and effective board provides appropriate oversight to staff and volunteers. Board members serve as our ambassadors, connecting us to our neighbors, and to other groups on the island.

SUMMARY, Whole Field Alignment in the ENVISION Phase

As the coach, in each step of the ENVISION phase, you will want to work with your client to:

Style:
- Increase deeply connected, positive conversations.

- Redefine *leadership* as a positive conversation for building self-worth, hope and capability throughout the system.

- Embrace positive Style considerations in how they act in relationships with customers, direct reports, family, stakeholders and others in their community.

Strategy:
- Commit to being open to coaching and choosing the positive as the focus of their inquiry.

- Develop a well-formed vision story; encourage co-creating it with system stakeholders to ensure it is widely spread.

- Build stakeholders' support for transformation.

- Identify and commit to their breakthrough.

- Incorporate into the vision a story about the contribution they're making and want to be making.

Structure:
- Construct a process for effective envisioning that results in a well-formed vision story.

- Engage the whole system in sharing the vision story.

- Work from a Whole Field perspective, identifying the system's stakeholders and integrating their stories into the client's vision story.

ALIGN

**The Future is
Now**

ALIGN PHASE

In the ALIGN Phase the coaching intention is to close the gap between the future the client yearns for, and their present reality.

In the LEAD Process, the ALIGN Phase is where the first draft of the Statements of Possibility (these were created in the ENVISION Phase) is finalized and applied.

This finalized version of the Statements of Possibility is the client's map and guide to the future, the basis for linking the desired ideal to everyday actions in the present. As the coach, you will resource your client by having them declare their committed intention to live day-to-day as if their imagined future was occurring here and now.

The actions of the ALIGN Phase should also be included as part of the annual governance cycle. If the vision changes, leaders will likely need to realign the organization's operating systems with it, and lead the system in a new direction.

Aligning may entail communication with stakeholders to share in and co-create the new vision, strategic intention setting and developing new strategies, aligning internal business operations and processes during an Operations Alignment

Review, following the recommendations of a LEAD TEAM, and training Process Works Study Teams to use Process Alignment Tools to align internal processes.

There are six components in the ALIGN Phase. While all six components of the ALIGN Phase are designed to stimulate change in the whole field, each component is most closely associated with changes that can be brought about in a specific WFA Field Inquiry arena (Style, Strategy or Structure).

1. **FRAME THE CONVERSATION (change in the system's Style)**

2. **STRENGTHEN THE CORE: self-worth, hope and capability (change in the system's Style)**

3. **TELL YOUR VISION STORY (change in the system's Strategy)**

4. **GENERATE POSSIBILITY (change in the system's Strategy)**

5. **ALIGN OPERATIONS and ESTABLISH A LEAD TEAM (change in the system's Structure)**

6. **TEACH PROCESS ALIGNMENT (change in the system's Structure)**

For a system, this will be a time of reinvention, when your ALIGN Phase coaching will include identifying the actions that should occur in each of the three components of Style, Strategy and Structure for there to be Whole Field Alignment. For example:

Action in the Style Frame might include a significant conversation shift, both internal and external, regarding self-worth, hope and capability (see the *Leadership for a Healthy World model* in Part One), and how to increase positive perspective.

Action in the Strategy Frame may include clarifying the client's view of the future, declaring the strategic positive possibilities, and identifying the methods that will be used to work towards acting as if that future is happening now.

In the Structure Frame, actions might include how the client intends to organize (reorganize) and align (realign) components of its system to achieve positive internal and customer engagement and how to implement structures that ensure sustainability of the change process.

During the ALIGN Phase, your coaching will also highlight the ways in which your client is <u>already</u> living their future ideal in their daily life, something you will explore further with them during the DELIVER Phase.

SUMMARY, Whole Field Alignment in the ALIGN Phase

As the coach, in each step of the ALIGN phase, you will want to work with your clients to:

Style:
- Increase the system-wide ALIGN conversation by asking, "What are you seeing, hearing or experiencing that demonstrates an increase in alignment with our vision story?"
- Model how to effectively apply the components of ALIGN such as framing the conversation, reframing to expand limits and become open to healthier beliefs, and strengthening the core of self-worth, hope and capability.
- Ask and answer, "What is already working and aligned?"

Strategy:
- Model how to effectively apply the components of ALIGN such as telling their vision story and generating possibility.
- Build skills is generating Statements of Possibility to bring the future into the present.
- Work with all their stakeholders' in creating a shared vision story.

Structure:
- Model how to effectively apply the components of ALIGN such as hold Operations Alignment Reviews and establishing a LEAD TEAM.
- Apply Process Alignment Tools to resolve process flow issues.
- Be open to restructuring to increase utilization of employee skills.
- Engage in a conversation, or conversations, about how to sustain the Whole Field Alignment changes.

DELIVER

Living into
Shared Vision

DELIVER PHASE

This is the phase for the unfolding of the future vision into daily practice. The guiding phrases would be, "What can I do more of to make my life and work even more vital and alive? What aspect of my work right now matches my vision? What is giving me a sense of self-worth, hope and capability?" And finally, "What do I need to do to align daily life with my vision?"

During the DELIVER Phase the coach checks in with the client at intervals, asking some of the following questions:

- What have you done that has worked?

- What would you do more of to make your life and work even more vital and alive, perhaps even beyond your wildest expectations?

- Who else needs to be involved to support you in achieving your vision?

- What other resources do you need to access?

- What would you want to explore further in support of bringing your dream into the present?

- On a scale of 1 – 4, what level of commitment and energy are you putting into achieving your breakthrough?

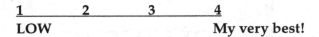

1   2   3   4
LOW   My very best!

- To what level are your stakeholders committed?

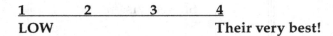

1   2   3   4
LOW   Their very best!

- What will you do to renew your commitment and take your energy to the next level?

- What will you do to renew your stakeholders in their commitment and help them take their energy to the next level?

LEAD TEAM ACTION during the DELIVER Phase: developing the five competencies

Coaching best practice includes creating a special charter for leaders to be accountable for guiding the system through the DELIVER Phase. This is organized and made possible through the implementation of the LEAD TEAM structure.

Implementing a LEAD TEAM involves assigning accountability for alignment and delivery to a group of experienced, committed people representing all levels and parts of the system. Those invited to be part of the LEAD TEAM utilize a competency-based framework to guide the system that is going through significant personal or organizational change. Being a part of a LEAD TEAM builds accountability, capability and leadership commitment across all divisions and levels within a business system, keeping people in the organization focused on achieving their breakthrough results over time.

Restructuring to create a LEAD TEAM involves bringing together

- The current leadership team (direct reports to the CEO, COO, Administrator, Business Owner, or Team Leader), and

- A selected group of individuals, usually one from all sections of the organization, who have already shown informal leadership. This LEAD TEAM takes on the accountability for Operations Alignment and the building of a system that is directed from its vision. Their goal is to bring the envisioned future (which was previously declared in the Statements of Possibility) into the present.

I call the process that will guide a LEAD TEAM *LEAD TEAM ACTION*. It has two parts.

During **Part one of LEAD TEAM ACTION,** the group forms the LEAD TEAM, and defines the five critical competencies of effective individuals, teams and large groups that are needed for creating a fully aligned system. These are:

Generative Competence
The ability of organizations and their members to learn from their experience and apply that knowledge in new situations.

Affirmative Competence
The ability to focus on what the organization and the individuals in it have done or are doing well, their strengths, successes, positive intentions, and potential.

Collaborative Competence
The ability to create forums in which all members can explore ideas, innovate, challenge assumptions, partner and interact in the pursuit of a common vision.

Catalytic Competence
The ability of organizations and their members to see and think beyond "reasonable" limits or familiar patterns; to commit to stretching their boundaries and challenging the status quo.

Whole Field Harmonizing Competence
The ability to capitalize on the interactive and interdependent
nature of whole systems, while engaging the system with respect
for oneself and others. Finding the points of intersection of ideas,
beliefs, desires and hopes.[80]

Developing these competencies builds a system-wide foundation for increasing
Whole System *IQ*.

Part two of LEAD TEAM ACTION provides LEAD TEAM members with
ideas on what they need to do to move their organizations in the direction of
becoming more highly functioning, capable and 'leader-full' (having empowered people) – and aligned with its Vision Story. In this part, the LEAD TEAM
reviews a listing of suggested actions from which an accountable LEAD TEAM
member might choose for how to engage others in conversations, projects, alignment teams or tasks that bring the future ideal into the present.

One important reason for using the LEAD TEAM structure is that it will develop this group into becoming internal change agents focused on the entire
field, rather than on the pieces each individual faces operationally day-to-day.
The LEAD TEAM will have the direction and tools required for more comprehensively identifying the support needed to implement and sustain whole field
transformation.

**For the complete guide to LEAD TEAM ACTION, see the Addendum, be-
ginning on page 187.**

The Timeline for Tomorrow: Putting LEAD into an ALIGN Coaching, whole field change process

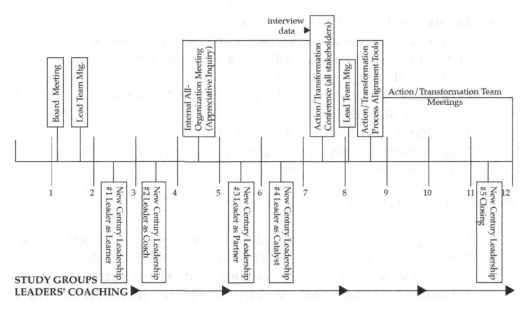

To conclude our discussion of LEAD and how to engage as a master coach in this component of ALIGN Coaching, I want to illustrate the application of LEAD in a whole field coaching intervention. The above "Timeline for Tomorrow," diagram illustrates a year-long coaching process I used with one of my clients who applied LEAD within their ALIGN Coaching change process.

This intervention design, much like the one given earlier in Part Two of this book (the "Timeline for Whole Field Change"), incorporates the idea of utilizing multiple-entries to ensure the whole field is engaged in the change process as much as possible. As stated before, multiple-entry is intended to create a critical mass for change by implementing changes throughout the system simultaneously.

In this version of the Timeline, each rectangle represents one entry (or contact point) of various stakeholder groups within the organization. Designed to transform the whole field during the year of the change process, the gatherings included:

SHOWN ABOVE THE LINE:

- Meetings with the Board of Directors
- An internal large-scale conference of all internal stakeholders (whole system in-the-room), here formatted as an Appreciative Inquiry[81]
- An external large-scale conference (called an Action /Transformation Conference) where all internal and external stakeholders were involved
- LEAD TEAM meetings
- PROCESS ALIGNMENT TOOLS Trainings
- Process Works Study Team meetings, (referred to here as "Action/ Transformation Team Meetings)

SHOWN BELOW THE LINE

- Ongoing coaching, including establishing an internal Coaching Program
- Formation of Study-Groups which held brown-bag lunch discussions
- Educational sessions of a custom-designed training program called "New Century Leadership," which was initially held for LEAD TEAM members plus board and executive leaders. Later the educational sessions were offered to all employees, taught by LEAD TEAM members (trained by the coach)

LEARN

In this design, after one-on-one coaching, the CEO, who was the initiating client, held LEARN Phase interviews with her direct reports and with other stakeholders and even with her family. The Board was also engaged in interviews with the CEO, and a version took place during their first Board Meeting. Getting the go-ahead from the Board, LEARN interviews were held with those attending the New Century Leadership program, and then extended to others in the Internal Conference's Appreciative Inquiry. Some aspects of LEARN interviewing were incorporated into the Action/Transformation Conference design, as well.

ENVISION

After working with her coach to imagine a well-formed vision, the CEO chose to share her vision story with the participants in the New Century Leadership program. Together with the program participants, preparations were made to design a vision process for internal stakeholders attending the Appreciative Inquiry, and then for the CEO to share her own vision story at the end of that day. Gaining clarity on their vision story was a key agenda for the Action/Transformation Conference where all stakeholders were present.

ALIGN

The agenda for the Action/Transformation Conference was concentrated on alignment, including gaining agreement on many aspects of the organization's life such as their core strengths and values. The ultimate goals was to align on their vision story. In closing, the internal and external stakeholders also engaged in identifying arenas where alignment of the vision with daily work was still needed and set priorities for addressing this.

DELIVER

In DELIVER, the LEAD TEAM met to organize to engage stakeholders in aligning various processes with the vision story. Priorities were set and both internal and external stakeholders were invited to participate in teams to study the selected processes, applying whole field alignment lenses, and propose a WFA approach to aligning them. This is the ongoing work of the LEAD TEAM, with the CEO and executive team's blessing and intention to resource redesigns of processes as needed.

SUMMARY, Whole Field Alignment in the DELIVER Phase

As the coach, in each part of the DELIVER phase, you will want to work with your clients to:

Style:
- Continue to frame the organization's conversation by asking, "What are you seeing, hearing or experiencing in a new more positive, hopeful and unlimited way?"
- Model using reframing effectively. Build client skills in positive reframing from breakdowns to breakthroughs.
- Resource your clients.
- Assist clients in building on their successes.
- Increase their sense of self-worth, hope and capability.
- Ask them, "What is already working and aligned?"

Strategy:
- Build stakeholder support.
- Develop a system-wide communication strategy to communicate their commitment to deliver.
- Explore the path toward delivery, basing it on the client's strengths.
- Extend the individual/organization Vision Story out into the whole system.

Structure:
- Build system capability by implementing LEAD TEAM ACTION, an expansion of leadership accountability for everyday actions towards achieving the vision.
- Extend creating teams knowledgeable in Process Alignment Tools, to resolve process flow issues.
- Be open to restructuring to increase utilization of employee skills.
- Engage in a conversation, or conversations, about how well the job fits the person's gifts and talents.

Your ALIGN Coaching goal: Creating Healthy Whole Systems

How do you know you are on the path to truly making a difference with your coaching? To really helping clients make a difference by creating the healthy, whole systems they yearn to be a part of?

Perhaps both you *and* your clients are complete with the limited approaches that have been used in previous coaching engagements. They don't work, and they don't last. As with any significant change, however, embracing ALIGN Coaching may require you to transform your practice and the way you think about who you are.

But while it might be a lot of front-end work, it will be nourishing work, both sacred and magical.

Is it time to talk with your clients about the possibilities that will come from taking a whole field perspective, and the outcomes they will achieve with ALIGN Coaching? As part of closing, I give you the final checklist, "A Checklist for Well-Formed, Whole Field Change," that can be used as part of those life-changing decisions – yours and theirs.

THE CHECKLIST FOR WELL-FORMED, WHOLE FIELD CHANGE

The ALIGN Coaching Guide to CREATING HEALTHY WHOLE SYSTEMS

A change is said to be well-formed if it

☐ Considers and involves the whole system.

☐ Is positive, bold and compelling.

☐ Shifts attention to the future.

☐ Disrupts the status quo.

☐ Is grounded in the system's strengths and deeply-held values.

☐ Points to evidence that demonstrates prior successes.

☐ Is inclusive.

☐ Is passionately desired.

☐ Supports ongoing learning about how to be what you always wanted to be.

"Service on behalf of the future is the essence of legacy. In this sense we are obliged to serve as midwife and torchbearer ... as well as tend the hearth of our own calling."

– Gloria Burgess[82]

In Closing

How the dream of the future sparked my everyday life.

For the past year and a half, every time I sat down at my computer to write this book, I was living my dream. I imagined myself creating a rich and valued legacy for those who embrace coaching as the means for positively influencing our world. Embracing that vision awakened me and excited me, and kept me in my chair for hours on end. It often woke me up at two a.m. with some new insight on how to put this guidebook together.

It shouldn't be surprising that this book is about how to align everyday life with one's vision. I lived the ideas in writing this book every day. And as with all efforts to live one's dream, writing this has been a joy and a challenge.

As *ALIGN, a Coach's Guide* was taking form I became increasingly aware of and pleased with the extent of the wisdom gained in my years of teaching and coaching that I wanted to pass on to others. I have mentored many coaches in my lifetime of coaching practice, and I saw this as a way to continue my commitment to being a mentor. And I am still open to having my coach coach me, as my dream includes being a life-long learner.

I am especially thrilled at the creative breakthrough I had that led to the coming together into one unified theory the ideas I began exploring more than twenty-five years ago. Those ideas, nascent back then, but much more fully formed now, comprise what I believe is an important contribution to our coaching community.

ALIGN, a Coach's Guide celebrates the results of my learning journey and the commitment to pass on my knowledge to colleagues, students, leaders and the next generation of coaches.

ADDENDUM

For those seeking Mastery of Whole System Coaching/ Mastery of ALIGN Coaching Certification

In the International Mastery of Coaching Certification (IMCC) programs that I have led for the past 25 years, we used the Five Competency framework as a means for participants to self-assess their **Readiness to Coach**.

This is aligned with my belief that as coaches we need to be as competent as our clients in being Generative, Affirmative, Collaborative, Catalytic and Whole Field Harmonizing. We need to know ourselves to the extent that we are confident in our ability to apply master coaching skills in Whole System *IQ* interventions.

I include here one of the Readiness to Coach self-assessments that was used in IMCC. At the end of the program, each participant scored themselves on the form that follows, and then completed a Readiness to Coach application. The teaching team met with each applicant to review and substantiate assessment.

You may want to read through the self-assessment that follows to get a sense of your own competencies as a master coach.

This checklist may also be useful to review before engaging the client, so that, as a coach, you are reminded of the work that is before you: to be present with the client, to show empathy, to practice immediacy, to speak the truth, to focus on the positive, to seek to deepen the conversation and to help your client take the next step.

READINESS TO COACH CHECKLIST & REQUEST FOR MASTERY OF COACHING CERTIFICATION

I am ready to coach my clients' through Whole System Positive-Core Change because I have demonstrated the following competencies.

Generative Competence is the ability to learn from experience and apply that knowledge to new situations. Not only is the task accomplished, but creative potential and innovative thinking are expanded as well.

The coach/consultant/leader with this capability creates a context in which inquiry and learning flourish. By encouraging awareness and flexibility in thinking and action, the conditions are created for your clients to respond to new challenges and change.

Focus: Awareness, Learning and Resilience, Innovating

☐ Provide ongoing support AND challenge for my clients/client systems, encouraging them to strive to achieve their stretch goals and to learn from their experience.

☐ Use multiple paths towards helping my client/client system achieve their breakthrough declarations.

☐ Check (and re-check) to be sure that my client is committed to their declared breakthrough. I am open to revising their breakthrough declaration if their commitments have changed.

☐ Am flexible and able to shift perspective to increase the possibility for new learning to occur.

Affirmative Competence is the ability to focus on what the client/client system has done or is doing well – the strengths, successes, positive intentions and potential of your client/client system.

The coach/consultant/leader with this capability celebrates achievements and strengths. By encouraging more empowering views of reality and by setting positive expectations of competence and success, s/he shapes behavior and opens up new possibilities within the system.

Focus: Acknowledgment, Renewal, Empowerment

☐ Engage in acknowledging and encouraging my clients to shift towards positive, whole field change. Model positive conversation and seeing the positive in myself and others.

☐ Show respect for the client/client system's perceptions and unique needs. I integrate and build on client/client system's ideas and suggestions.

☐ Celebrate the client/client system for its strengths, and use identified strengths as a basis for moving into new arenas for empowerment.

☐ Support clients/client systems in discovering new approaches, constructive beliefs and values, and being open to new perceptions and feelings that strengthen their ability to take action, while minimizing looking backwards to past failures or negative experiences.

Collaborative Competence is the ability to create forums in which all clients and members of the client system can explore ideas, challenge assumptions, partner and interact in the pursuit of common goals and new ideas.

The coach/consultant/ leader with this capability designs organization structures that encourage active debate and the championing of many perspectives and ideas—a continuous, open, active dialogue, that contributes to effectiveness in relationships and positive partnering.

Focus: Commitment, Partnership, Communication

☐ Collaborate with my client in envisioning the ideal future and creating Statements of Possibility. Ensure that clients "own" their part in moving toward the future state.

☐ Ensure there is collaboration and involvement of stakeholders in the change process.

☐ Invoke co-inquiry for greater understanding and awareness, achieved through diverse perspectives.

☐ Am able to distinguish trivial from significant issues, focusing the collaborative inquiry on the most important issues the client/client system needs to address.

Catalytic Competence is the ability to see and think beyond "reasonable" limits or familiar patterns; to commit to stretching one's boundaries and to achieving results by inquiring into emerging possibilities.

Coaches/consultants/leaders with this capability make it "safe" to redefine boundaries and to experiment with new ideas for achieving results that contribute to healthy systems. They are catalysts for wide-ranging conversations within the system, in the community and in the global village, that lead to innovative ways of thinking and organizing.

Focus: Shared Vision, Operations and Process Alignment

☐ Coach clients into initiating a co-creative relationship with and within a chartered LEAD TEAM, accountable for having a whole system view of the change process, and empowered to make recommendations to senior leadership. Facilitate their first meeting.

☐ Identify for the client/client system any rigid and unhelpful ways of perceiving and reframe them to create a broader perspective and new openings for action and engagement.

☐ Utilize the language of breakthrough to positive possibilities to awaken the client to ways to close the gap between the desired future state and the present. Encourage the client to act "as if" the future is now.

<u>Whole Field Harmonizing Competence</u> is the ability to understand the whole system, and to engage the system with respect for oneself, others, the community and the world. This includes holding a view that is inclusive and open to learning from others, recognizing and experiencing the world from another's point of view – an emotional resonance much like "walking in another person's shoes".

A coach/consultant/leader with this capability sees his or her connection to the whole system, even to the global community, and seeks to engage ecologically and empathetically at every level of system. He or she recognizes the value of eliminating boundaries between people and systems, and encourages inclusion of a broad range of inputs.

Focus: Ecology, Whole Field Alignment, Sustainability, Whole Community Respect

☐ Apply WS *IQ* and WFA in assessing and intervening in the client's system, and in evaluating the impact of system changes on its internal and external communities.

☐ Encourage mentoring and other forms of leadership development, involving both internal and external stakeholders.

☐ Consider system ecology/fit when helping clients develop a shared vision, breakthrough declarations, and positive possibilities, to ensure well-formed conditions are met, and the sustainability of the change effort.

Mastering the Whole Field Change process, and one's self.

I . . .

- ☐ Follow the carefully designed WS *IQ*, Whole Field Alignment and LEAD processes when coaching my clients.

- ☐ Ask questions that evoke discovery, insight, commitment or new action, championing new behavior and appropriate risk-taking.

- ☐ Work effectively with strong emotions, self-managing and maintaining a viewpoint from outside the system while remaining 100% committed to my client/client system's breakthrough Statements of Possibility.

- ☐ Am present in the moment (immediacy), open to my intuition and inner knowing, and model this for my clients/client systems.

- ☐ Recognize the positive intention behind negative communication and reframe it for my clients.

- ☐ Acknowledge the inducting power of systems and get coaching for myself.

The author would like to acknowledge the contributions of Frank Barrett to an earlier version of this model of competencies for effective leaders, coaches and consultants.

ADDENDUM

LEAD TEAM ACTION GUIDE

Directions:

Make a copy of the following LEAD TEAM ACTION GUIDE for each member of the LEAD TEAM and hand it out during the start-up meeting.

A one or two-day ORIENTATION for LEAD TEAM members is recommended, preferably held offsite.

"If your actions inspire others to dream more, learn more, do more and become more, you are a leader."

– John Quincy Adams

LEAD TEAM ACTION GUIDE

ALIGN AND DELIVER THROUGH SHARED LEADERSHIP.

LEAD TEAM ACTION is a structure that is used for assigning accountabilities and tasks to support aligning day-to-day practices with vision.

LEAD TEAM ACTION is a framework used for guiding the actions of leaders and members of systems that are going through significant personal or organizational change. To ensure the sustainability of the system's change process and the positive, attitudes, beliefs and values that were embraced by members of your organization, a group representing all divisions of the organization was selected to be an adjunct to the executive and management team. You are here because you were asked to volunteer to bring to the LEAD TEAM your skills, experience and knowledge so that each organizational unit will be well represented.

"Leadership is the capacity to translate vision into reality," Warren Bennis, a pioneer in leadership studies, once stated.[1] The work of leaders in a system is to establish the vision, set direction and clarify what matters, while managers ensure that promised work gets completed. The LEAD TEAM, as an adjunct

---

[1] Bennis, W. (2009), *On Becoming a Leader*, Perseus Books, Philadelphia, PA.

leadership team, is focused solely on alignment of the system with its vision and makes recommendations on what to do to move with confidence towards alignment.

The LEAD TEAM consults. Final decisions to support a recommendation rest with the organization's leaders and managers.

Restructuring to create a LEAD TEAM involves bringing together

a) The current leadership team (The CEO, COO, Administrator, Business Owner or Team Leader and their direct reports) and

b) A select group of individuals, usually one person from each section of the organization. For the purposes of the LEAD TEAM, this diverse group should be composed of people who have already shown informal leadership and who are committed to the vision.

The LEAD TEAM, while accountable for aligning operations with vision, works through others. You may even form a subcommittee to inquire more deeply into an issue. Your executive leadership team may ask you to take on projects, charter a Process Works Study Team, or make recommendations to them regarding changes in rewards for employees. You are likely to be exposed to new learning and be asked to build positive relationships throughout the entire organization.

Whatever you do, please remember that your goal is to bring the envisioned future into the present, initiating and sustaining being the future now.

This LEAD TEAM ACTION Guide has two sections.

Section one of this LEAD TEAM ACTION GUIDE identifies and defines the five critical competencies of effective individuals, teams and groups that are needed for creating a fully aligned organization. Developing these competencies builds a system-wide foundation for increasing whole system capacity.

Section two of the LEAD TEAM ACTION GUIDE provides ideas and specific examples of what you and members of your LEAD TEAM could do to move your organization in the direction of becoming more highly functioning, capable and 'leader-full' (having empowered people) – and becoming aligned with its vision. This section contains a listing of suggested actions from which an accountable LEAD TEAM might choose, for how to engage others in tasks or conversations that bring the future ideal into the present.

Working with the LEAD TEAM ACTION framework will allow your organization to produce results more quickly and efficiently, and to build resilience and agility for dealing with change.

SECTION 1

LEAD TEAM overall purpose: Whole Field Alignment

With coaching support, the LEAD TEAM is chartered to guide efforts to align the system with its vision. They do this by focusing on building organizational competency in key operational areas so that the vision starts showing up in employees' day-to-day actions.

Research has shown that there are five competencies needed by an organization's leaders, members and stakeholders for creating an aligned, positive, empowered and productive system. Leaders, teams, individuals and organizations that are responsive to changes in their environment, and are able to produce and sustain impressive results, demonstrate competence in these five arenas:

1) **Generative Competence**

2) **Affirmative Competence**

3) **Collaborative Competence**

4) **Catalytic Competence**

5) **Whole Field Harmonizing Competence**

The LEAD TEAM takes on accountability for building these competencies.

1. Generative Competence: Resilience and Learning

Generative Competence is the ability to learn from experience and apply that knowledge to new situations. Thus, not only is the task accomplished, but creative potential and innovative thinking are expanded as well.

The LEAD TEAM creates a context in which inquiry and learning flourish by encouraging awareness and flexibility in thinking and action, and the conditions for responsiveness to new challenges, innovation and change.

2. Affirmative Competence: Acknowledgement and Renewal

Affirmative Competence is the ability to focus on what the system and the individuals in it have done or are doing well – their strengths, successes, positive core, positive intentions and potential – with the larger commitment to build a sense of self-worth, hope and capability.

The LEAD TEAM builds this capability by encouraging the organization to celebrate achievements and strengths. By having more empowering views of reality and by setting positive expectations of competence and success, the LEAD TEAM can shape behavior, create hope, and open up new possibilities within the system.

3. Collaborative Competence: Commitment and Partnering

Collaborative Competence is the ability to create forums in which all members can explore ideas, challenge assumptions, partner and interact in the pursuit of common goals and new ideas.

The individual, team, leader or organization with this capability designs structures that encourage active debate and the championing of many perspectives and ideas–– a continuous, open, active dialogue, that contributes to effectiveness in relationships and positive partnering. By working together, the LEAD TEAM sets up a model from which to set standards for collaboration throughout the system.

4. Catalytic Competence: Connecting in the Community

Catalytic Competence is the ability to stretch beyond "reasonable" limits, familiar patterns or old boundaries, especially in relationships, sparking breakthrough results via having an engaged community inquiring into emerging possibilities.

The individual, team, leader or organization with this capability shares their vision and makes it "safe" to redefine boundaries, and to experiment with new ideas for achieving results that contribute to healthy systems. The LEAD TEAM serves as a catalyst for wide-ranging conversations with stakeholders within the organization, in the community and in the global village, that lead to innovative ways of thinking and organizing.

5. Whole Field Harmonizing Competence: Global Whole Field Alignment

Whole Field Harmonizing Competence is the ability to understand and integrate the whole field in order to work and live in harmony. The LEAD TEAM helps establish a climate of respect for themselves, others, the community and the world. This includes holding a view that is inclusive and open to learning from others, recognizing and experiencing the world from another's point of view, and having an emotional resonance much like "walking in another person's shoes".

To do this the LEAD TEAM will ensure that system members see their connection to the global community and seek to engage ecologically and empathetically at every level of system. They will promote the value of diversity and eliminating boundaries between people and systems, and encourage inclusion of a broad range of people, their ideas and thoughtful inputs.

SECTION 2

LEAD TEAM engages in assessing and building competencies.

Section 2 of LEAD TEAM ACTION lists the five competencies and links them to those aspects of organizational life on which a LEAD TEAM might focus. A guiding "Purpose" for those engaged in that focus is given.

Finally, in the "Overview" that follows, some specific elements of organization life are listed. These are intended to serve as a starting place for inquiry.

Experience has shown that this intense focus will be needed to move your system in the direction of becoming more aligned, more highly functioning, capable, 'leader-full,' and empowered. You will serve as a guiding coalition in support of leadership to ensure the achievement of your organization's break-through possibilities.

You are encouraged to follow your passion in the selection of a competency arena on which to focus. In addition to the suggestions given here, LEAD TEAM members may customize the list for their arena of focus by adding particulars that might be specific to your own system.

You will

- Understand and assess your selected arena of focus;

- Brainstorm and research others' (other systems, companies, departments or team's) successes;

- Study the various possibilities, test to be sure they are aligned with your organization's vision, and make recommendations to your leadership group on what needs to be done.

The timeframe for commitment to be active on the LEAD TEAM will be one year, with an opportunity to extend your participation to two years. There will be a rotating schedule for replacement.

At the end of the first year, you will be asked to evaluate how far the system has come in becoming what it wants to be, while pointing toward how you might complete its journey to the future.

The following is a listing of the five competencies and their associated focus arenas. For each focus arena there is a suggested "purpose" and an "overview".

In the "Overview", some specific parts of organization life are bulleted. This list should point to a place where the investigations/inquiries of the LEAD TEAM can get started.

Focus Arenas for LEAD TEAM to Explore

Each of the five competencies is linked with three Focus Arenas. Evidencing positive changes in these in organizational life becomes the LEAD TEAM Action agenda.

Generative Competence:
> Awareness
> Learning/Resilience
> Innovating

Affirmative Competence:
> Acknowledgment
> Renewal
> Empowerment

Collaborative Competence:
> Commitment
> Partnership
> Alignment

Catalytic Competence:
> Creativity
> Strength-based Inquiry
> Shared Vision

Whole Field Harmonizing Competence:
> Ecology
> Sustainability
> Inclusiveness/ Empathy/Community Respect

1. **To build <u>GENERATIVE COMPETENCE</u>, select a LEAD TEAM member(s) to focus on:**

AWARENESS
LEARNING/RESILIENCE
INNOVATING

Purpose:

- To develop education and communications processes that keep people informed about the plans and status of the organization's efforts to grow and change.

- To establish learning as a top priority and encourage the conditions that allow for continuous learning.

- To give people the knowledge and skills required to participate effectively. To get information into the hands of those who need and can use it.

Overview

Addressing Awareness, Learning and Resilience, and Innovating involves focusing on these key elements:

- Employee and stakeholder orientation.

- Communication.

- Creating a learning organization.

- Conditions allowing for Innovation

2. To build <u>AFFIRMATIVE COMPETENCE</u>, select a LEAD TEAM member(s) to focus on:

ACKNOWLEDGMENT
RENEWAL
EMPOWERMENT

Purpose:

- To demonstrate commitment to the future, while valuing the past; to let what's working guide improvement efforts.

- To build a culture of acknowledgement, empowerment and partnership, and make the changes needed in recognition and reward systems to support it.

- To create an environment in which people can contribute their best by identifying and clarifying pathways for communicating new ideas and giving input to decisions.

- To celebrate and publicly acknowledge progress and results, bringing renewed energy and fun to everyday operations.

- To ensure that employees experience having choices and possibilities, rather than limitations, as well as the freedom to engage in appropriate alternatives.

- To reflect in your speaking and listening your commitment to empowering others.

Overview

The key elements for focus in Acknowledgment, Renewal and Empowerment are:

- Change the conversation towards the positive, so you are focusing on strengths.

- Evaluate recognition and reward systems, and evaluate policies, procedures and work operations, revising them to allow for participation and choice.

- Open new channels for communication and ask for input into decisions.

- Encourage self-reflection.

- Celebrate what is working.

3. To build **<u>COLLABORATIVE COMPETENCE</u>**, select a **LEAD TEAM** member(s) to focus on:

COMMITMENT
PARTNERSHIP
COMMUNICATION

Purpose:

- To redefine partnership as a strategic opportunity and develop partnering capability throughout the organization.

- To establish the structures and roles necessary for creating and supporting a new culture that legitimizes responsible action, participation, inquiry and continuous learning, coaching, and partnering.

- To examine and change one's personal actions and leadership behaviors which are inconsistent with a commitment to partnership.

- To develop a vehicle for involvement and commitment that allows you to engage as partners in co-constructing the organization and its culture.

- To encourage those who have resisted or not believed in the viability of the organization to become involved in supporting your efforts.

Overview

Commitment, Partnership and Alignment require a system to:

- Remove any barriers to commitment and develop structures that allow for responsibility and participation.

- Model partnership. Examine leaders' actions and communications relative to their impact on partnering.

- Develop and apply new skills for generating commitment and partnership.

- Align structures to facilitate partnering at all levels, and with external stakeholders as well.

- Support teamwork within and across each area of the organization and in community interactions.

- Begin a system-wide conversation about what further possibilities there are for even greater committed partnering and resourcefulness, and for being resources to one another.

4. To build <u>CATALYTIC COMPETENCE</u>, select a LEAD TEAM member(s) to focus on:

CREATIVITY
STRENGTH-BASED INQUIRY
SHARED VISION

Purpose:

- To involve employees and other stakeholders in identifying the organization's core values and in dreaming its future.

- To articulate the 'stretch' this new future implies and model the willingness to learn and grow.

- To envision and articulate the possibilities of the future (Statements of Possibility) and begin aligning operations and processes to achieve it.

- To ensure that everyone understands the key areas targeted for results and develop an implementation plan against which progress can be measured.

Overview

To build Creativity, Strength-based Inquiry and Shared Vision:

- Sponsor a forum for articulating the opportunity of the future.

- Plan the process of aligning internal operations and procedures with the compelling future vision.

- Identify and focus on a limited number of specific financial goals, and clearly communicate expectations for achieving those goals.

- Develop a positive method for tracking and reporting progress and outcomes.

5. **To build <u>WHOLE FIELD HARMONIZING COMPETENCE</u>, select a LEAD TEAM member(s) to focus on:**

ECOLOGY & SUSTAINABILITY
WHOLE FIELD ALIGNMENT
WHOLE COMMUNITY RESPECT

Purpose:

- To increase the level of Whole System Intelligence and Whole Field Alignment in order to ensure sustainable, ecological development.

- To build healthy communities and a compassionate world by eliminating system barriers and conflict and enhancing relationships.

- To maintain high ethical standards in external and internal relationships which contribute to respect; to demonstrate confidence in others' capabilities and practice positive regard.

- To develop sensitivity to the external forces affecting a system and become flexible and able to adjust to the environment in which the system operates; to become ecological.

- To generate compassion and ensure fairness worldwide by removing boundaries between individuals, teams, businesses, communities, social, political and financial categories, countries, and other human systems.

Overview

Ecology & Sustainability, Whole Field Alignment, and Whole Community Respect require

- In difficult conversations, account for the benefits to all partners, and of partnership itself, when framing issues; uncover shared interests, generate positive options, and hold present the possibility of forgiveness.

- Structure activities so that society, its members and its economies are able to meet their needs and express their greatest potential.

- Preserve human diversity, biodiversity and natural ecosystems by planning and acting to maintain them for the long term.

- Identify boundaries between systems and make all of these barriers much more permeable than they are now. De-layer the system. Connect people and processes.

- Let information, ideas, resources, and energy flow throughout the organization to others, wherever they are needed. Extinguish the "not invented here" conversation.

Sustaining change: a goal of LEAD TEAM ACTION

LEAD TEAM ACTION creates the opportunity to fundamentally reframe each person's philosophical stance towards being deliberately hopeful, working with optimism, creating opportunity, and celebrating the human spirit. As a structure for ensuring that the gains from the change process are delivered and that they are sustainable, LEAD TEAM ACTION is applicable in a wide range of businesses and in government, in the higher education sector and in schools, in healthcare organizations, with community agencies and in professional service firms, as an energizing and effective process for supporting complex planning, designing structural change, working collaboratively across business units, and engaging communities and external stakeholders in matters ranging from policy development to resource allocation.

In chartering this leadership group your clients are creating a collaborative partnership and constructing a new workplace culture, one that can go beyond problem-solving to identifying and building on core strengths. Growing bench strength in resilience, needed for agility in today's chaotic markets, is also an expected outcome.

Some results from organizations utilizing LEAD TEAM ACTION include:

- Improved cross-organization collaboration
- Strategic planning
- Post-merger integration
- Resolved communication issues
- The creation of a high performance culture
- Process Alignment
- Leadership and executive coaching
- Performance management

ENDNOTES

INTRODUCTION AND OVERVIEW

1   Private conversation with Dave Riddle, October 2019.

2   Mindell, A. (1995), *Sitting in the Fire*: *Large Group Transformation Using Conflict and Diversity*. Deep Democracy Exchange, San Francisco, CA.

3   Trevor, J and Varcoe, B (2017) "How Aligned is your Organization," *Harvard Business Review*, Feb. 2017.

4   Block, P. (2000), *Flawless Consulting, 2nd Edition*. Jossey-Bass Pfeiffer, San Francisco.

5   Terkel, S. (1974), *Working*, Ballatine Books, N.Y.

6   Kotter, J. (1995), "Leading Change; Why Transformational Efforts Fail", *Harvard Business Review*, June-July 1995.

PART 1

7   George, B. (2007). *True North, discover your authentic leadership*, Jossey-Bass, Wiley, San Francisco, CA.

8   Connor, J. (2014). *Dreams to Action Trailblazer's Guide*, Pajudacon Press, US.

9   Peter Block, (2011), *Flawless Consulting*, John Wiley & Sons, San Francisco, CA.

10 Berquist, W. (1993). "The postmodern organization," *The International Journal of Coaching in Organizations*. Jossey-Bass, San Francisco, CA.

11 Watzlawick, P., Bavelas, J., & Jackson, D. (1967) *Pragmatics of Human Communication*, WW Norton, New York, NY

12 Fox, J. (2011) "What is it that Only I Can Do?" (Interview with John Mackey), *Harvard Business Review*, January – February 2011, Boston.

13 Tojo Thatchenkery, in *Affirmation as Intervention*, paper presented at the 1999 International Conference of Language in Organizational Change and Transformation. May 14-16. Max M. Fisher College of Business, Ohio State University, Columbus, Ohio.

14 Van Warmerdam, G. (2014), *Mindworks, A Practical Guide for Changing thoughts Beliefs and Emotional Reactions*, Cairn Publishing, Santa Barbara, CA.

15 Fox, J. (2011) "What is it that Only I Can Do?" (Interview with John Mackey), *Harvard Business Review*, January – February 2011, Boston.

16 See Dee Hock, *One From Many: Visa and the Rise of the Chaordic Organization*, Berrett-Koehler, San Francisco, CA. 2005.

See also David Cooperrider's "Forward" in *Conversations Worth Having*, by Stavros and Torres, Penguin/Random House.

17 https://www.instituteforcivility.org/who-we-are/what-is-civility/

18 Cooperrider, D. (1990). Positive Image, Positive Action, The Affirmative Basis of Organizing," in *Appreciative Management and Leadership, The Power of Positive Thought and Action in Organizations* by Suresh Srivastva, David L. Cooperrider, and Associates.

19 Covey, S. (2013), *The 7 Habits of Highly Effective People: Powerful Lessons in Personal Change*, Simon & Schuster, New York, NY.

20 Roberts, C. (1994) *The Fifth Discipline Fieldbook: Strategies and tools for building a learning organization*, (with Peter Senge, Art Kleiner, Rick Ross, Bryan Smith and George Roth), Crown/Archetype, Emmeryville, CA.

21 Nicholls, J. (1988). "Leadership in Organisations: meta, macro and micro." *European Management Journal*, Amsterdam.

22 Dilts, R. & Zolno, S. (1992)."Skills for the New Paradigm: lessons from Italy," *Organization Development*, American Society for Training and Development, Spring, 1992,Washington, DC.

23 Zolno, S. (2013). "Toward a Healthy World. Meeting the leadership challenges of the Twenty-first Century," *Pfeiffer Annual*, John Wiley & Sons: San Francisco, CA.

24 Dilts, R. & Zolno, S. (1992)."Skills for the New Paradigm: lessons from Italy," *Organization Development,* American Society for Training and Development, Spring, 1992, Washington, DC.

25 Gosss, T., Pascale, R., Athos, A. (1993). "The Reinvention Roller Coaster," *Harvard Business Review,* Nov.-Dec.

26 Webber, A. (2001). "How Business Is a Lot Like Life." *Fast Company,* April 2001.

27 Bushe, G.R. & Pitman, T. (1991) Appreciative Process: A method for transformational change. *OD Practitioner,* 23:3, 1-4.

28 Niemiec, R. and McGrath, R. (2019). *The Power of Character Strengths: Appreciate and Ignite Your Positive Personality.*

29 LEAD TEAM is a structure with an ongoing mandate to support leadership teams in creating healthy whole systems. LEAD TEAM members have accountability for developing system-wide self worth, hope and capability, and whole system competencies.

30 Anderson, G. (1996). The 22 Non-Negotiable Laws of Wellness. HarperCollins, NY.

31 Retrieved: https://www.tonyrobbins.com/tony-robbins-quotes/

32 Zolno, S. (2007), "Towards a Healthy World: Meeting the Challenges of the 21st Century," in *LINKAGES,* Issue 34, Summer 2007.

33 Skillman, R. and Zolno, S (2009). Excerpted from *Memoir of a CEO: Leading with Heart and Soul,* in *LINKAGES,* Kirkland, WA.

34 Huang, C. A. and Lynch, J. (1995) *Mentoring, The Tao of Giving and Receiving Wisdom,* Harper. San Francisco.

35 Branden, N. (1994). *The Six Pillars of Self Esteem,* Bantam Books, New York, NY.

36 Frank, J. (1993) *Persuasion and Healing: A Comparative Study of Psychotherapy,* Johns Hopkins University Press, Cambridge, MA.

37 Niebuhr, R. (1952), *The Irony of American History,* Charles Scribner's & Sons, The University of Chicago Press.

38 Hutson, H. & Perry, B. (2006). *Putting Hope to Work: Five principles to activate your organizations most powerful resource.* Praeger, Westport, CT.

39 Riddle, D. (2007). "Practitioner Theory," Paper submitted for review, Leadership Institute of Seattle, Bothell, WA.

40 IBID

41 Kouzes, J. and Posner, B. (1987). *The Leadership Challenge,* Jossey-Bass, San Francisco.

42 Alarcon, R. & Frank, J. editors (2012). *The Psychotherapy of Hope,* The Johns Hopkins University Press, Baltimore, MD.

43 Fox, J. (2011) "What is it that Only I Can Do?" (Interview with John Mackey), *Harvard Business Review,* January – February 2011, Boston.

44 Prayers of Rev. Peter Marshall, April 18, 1947, as Chaplain to the US Senate.

45 Retrieved: https://airandspace.si.edu/stories/editorial/we-choose-go-moon-and-other-apollo-speeches

46 Spoken by Brian Doyle in a workshop held at Seattle University, Spring, 2017.

47 Retrieved: https://airandspace.si.edu/stories/editorial/we-choose-go-moon-and-other-apollo-speeches

48 Senge, P. (1990) *The Fifth Discipline.* Doubleday, New York, NY.

49 Levin, Ira (2000). "Vision Revisited, Telling the Story of the Future," *The Journal of Applied Behavioral Science,* Vol 36, No. 1, March 2000.

50 IBID

51 Erickson, M & Rossi, E. (1976) "Two level communication and the microdynamics of trance." *American Journal of Clinical Hypnosis,* 18.

52 Retrieved from FSi Engineer's document, "2020 VISION". Used with permission of Rob Danforth, CEO, and Larry Ransom of Ransomvision, their coach. Modified by the author.

53 Zolno, S. (2010) "Inspiring a Shared Vision," in *The Leadership Challenge Activities Book*, reprinted with permission of The Leadership Challenge, A Wiley Brand. Used with author's permission.

54 Gilbert, E. (2015). *Big Magic*. Riverhead Books, New York, NY.

55 The author thanks Barbara Grace, from Medium, for the dominoes metaphor.

56 Cooperrider, D. (1990), "Positive Image, Positive Action: The Affirmative Basis of Organizing," in Srivastva, S. and Cooperrider, D. *Appreciative Management and Leadership*, Rev. Euclid, OH, Lakeshore Communications.

57 Harman, W. (1988), *Global Mind Change: The New Age Revolution in the Way We Think*, Warner Books, New York, NY.

58 Bandler, R. and Grinder, J. (1975) *Structure of Magic I and II*, Science and Behavior Books, Palo Alto, CA.

59 Altucher, J. (2017), *Choose Yourself*, Lioncrest Publishing, Austin, TX.

60 Goss, T, Pascale, R., Athos, A., (1993) "The Reinvention Roller Coaster," *Harvard Business Review*, November – December, Boston.

61 Bennis, W. (2009), *On Becoming a Leader*, Perseus Books, Philadelphia, PA.

62 Heifetz, R. (1994), *Leadership without Easy Answers*. Harvard University Press, MA.

63 Gosss, T., Pascale, R., Athos, A. (1993). "The Reinvention Roller Coaster," *Harvard Business Review*, Nov.-Dec.

PART 2

64 Conner, D. (1992), *Managing at the Speed of Change*. Random House, New York.

65 Simon, H. (1947). *Administrative Behavior*, 4th ed. in 1997, The Free Press.

66 Heifetz, R. (1994), *Leadership without Easy Answers*. Harvard University Press, MA.

67 Zolno, S. (2008). "Getting Smart About System Change," in *The 2008 Pfeiffer Annual*, John Wiley & Sons, Inc. San Francisco.

68 Zolno, S. (1987). "Critical Mass and Change: Taking on Big County," in American Society for Training and Development's *Theory to Practice. The Role of OD in Quality Management and Productivity Improvement*, ASTD, Washington DC.

69 Zolno, S. (2008). "Change Congruence. Achieving Critical Mass in Your Change Programs." Unpublished manuscript from her presentation for the American Society for Training and Development, Region 8 Conference.

Zolno, S. (1988). "Productivity Through OD: Taking On Big County," *The Role of Organization Development in Quality Management and Productivity Improvement*, University of Minnesota Research Center/ASTD, Alexandria, VA.

PART 3

70 Block, P. (2008). *Community. The structure of belonging*. Berrett-Koehler, San Francisco.

71 Zolno, S. (2002). "Appreciative Inquiry: New Thinking at Work," *The 2002 Annual: Developing Human Resources*, Jossey-Bass/Pfeiffer & Company, San Francisco.

72 Levin, Ira (2000). "Vision Revisited, Telling the Story of the Future, *The Journal of Applied Behavioral Science*, Mar 2000.

73 Nanus, B. (1992). *Visionary Leadership*. Jossey-Bass, Inc. San Francisco, CA.

74 I would like to acknowledge John McConnell for this insight.

75 Brown, John Seeley (2002), "Research That Reinvents the Corporation," *Harvard Business Review*. Boston, MA.

76 BL Fredrickson, MF Losada - American psychologist, 2005 - psycnet.apa.org

Abstract: Extending BL Fredrickson's (1998) broaden-and-build theory of positive emotions and M. Losada's (1999) nonlinear dynamics model of team performance, the authors predicted that a ratio of positive to negative affect at or above 2.9 characterized individuals in flourishing mental health.

77   Argyris, C. (1980) *Inner contradictions of rigorous research.* Academic Press, New York, NY.

78   Nanus, B. (1992) *Visionary Leadership: Creating a Compelling Sense of Direction for Your Organization.* Jossey-Bass Publishers, San Francisco, CA.

79   Zolno, S. (1988), "Crisis at Home: Fostering Agreement in an Intentional Community" *VisionAction Journal*, OD Network, San Francisco, CA.

80   I am grateful for the inspiration provided by Frank Barrett whose earlier version of a set of competencies was introduced in his article, *"Creating Appreciative Learning Cultures,"* in Organizational Dynamics, Autumn 1995. I have made several changes and additions resulting in this extended version.

81   Zolno, S. (2002). "Appreciative Inquiry: New Thinking at Work," *The 2002 Annual: Developing Human Resources,* Jossey-Bass/Pfeiffer & Company, San Francisco.

82   Burgess, G. (2009). "Legacy Leadership: the call to stewardship and service," in *Linkage*, LIOS Publications, Kirkland, WA.

Sherene Zolno

In demand as a public speaker, Sherene has introduced ALIGN and Whole System *IQ* to audiences around the globe, including at the Appreciative Inquiry International Conference (Nepal), the International OD Association Conference (Canada), the International Leadership Conference (Europe), the OD Network National Conference (US), Healthcare Strategies Conference (Asia), the Association for Humanistic Psychology (US), and The Spirit in Work Symposium (San Juan Islands).

An original thinker who is passionate about bringing motivating stories of health and well-being into the business world, she led the international design team that created the original APPRECIATIVE LEADERSHIP model (Leadership for a Healthy World). Her writing on Whole System *IQ* (Intelligence) has appeared in OD Network's *VisionAction* Journal, in Jossey-Bass/Pfeiffer's *Annuals*, in ASTD's *Research Monograph*, as well as in numerous other professional publications.

Sherene's distinguished history of service in community and professional organizations includes serving on ASTD's regional and national boards – earning her an Outstanding Contributor Award – and on a number of national and community boards, plus serving as a volunteer facilitator for appreciative visioning conversations in her community.

Sharon Zeiler

in demand as a public speaker, she co-authored and hosted AUDIO and WRITE systems (?) to all homes and led the global audience at an Appreciative Inquiry International Conference. (Pre-all the International OD Association Conference Canada), the International Consulting Conference (San ???), the OD Network National Conference (???) Healthcare, Sustainable ???), the Association for Humanistic (Washington D.C.), the Chrysalis In Work Symposium (San Juan Islands)

An original thinker who is passionate about organizational ??? of healthcare and well-being into ??? businesses value, she led the migration of ???, a firm that created an OnLINE WAY TREATING TERMS, a PhD model ??? for fashion technology. Work that may be ??? for Wh... for Exam to the ??? has appeared in OD Network, ??? Journal and ??? In Jones Press (Review), chapters in AGD's Resource Workshops, as well as ??? international professional publications.

She has a distinguished history of service to the community and professional organizations includes serving on ASTD's ??? ??? and chief national board, serving her an Outstanding Contribution Award and as a member of Executive and community involvements, plus serving on ??? and her biography ??? that has contributed conversation of her community.

Printed in the United States
By Bookmasters